RESPONDING TO LOSS AND BEREAVEMENT IN SCHOOLS

by the same author

Lost for Words
Loss and Bereavement Awareness Training
John Holland, Ruth Dance, Nic Macmanus and Carole Stitt
ISBN 978 1 84310 324 0
eISBN 978 1 84642 107 5

Understanding Children's Experiences of Parental Bereavement
John Holland
ISBN 978 1 84310 016 4
eISBN 978 1 84642 230 0

of related interest

Effective Grief and Bereavement Support
The Role of Family, Friends, Colleagues, Schools and Support Professionals
Kari Dyregrov and Atle Dyregrov
ISBN 978 1 84310 667 8
eISBN 978 1 84642 833 3

Grief in Children
A Handbook for Adults, Second Edition
Atle Dyregrov
ISBN 978 1 84310 612 8
eISBN 978 1 84642 781 7

Talking About Death and Bereavement in School
How to Help Children Aged 4 to 11 to Feel Supported and Understood
Ann Chadwick
ISBN 978 1 84905 246 7
eISBN 978 0 85700 527 4

Communicating with Children When a Parent is at the End of Life
Rachel Fearnley
ISBN 978 1 84905 234 4
eISBN 978 0 85700 475 8

Great Answers to Difficult Questions about Death
What Children Need to Know
Linda Goldman
ISBN 978 1 84905 805 6
eISBN 978 1 84642 957 6

Setting Up and Facilitating Bereavement Support Groups
A Practical Guide
Dodie Graves
ISBN 978 1 84905 271 9
eISBN 978 0 85700 573 1

RESPONDING TO LOSS AND BEREAVEMENT IN SCHOOLS

A TRAINING RESOURCE TO ASSESS, EVALUATE AND IMPROVE THE SCHOOL RESPONSE

JOHN HOLLAND

Jessica Kingsley *Publishers*
London and Philadelphia

First published in 2016
by Jessica Kingsley Publishers
73 Collier Street
London N1 9BE, UK
and
400 Market Street, Suite 400
Philadelphia, PA 19106, USA

www.jkp.com

Library of Congress Cataloging in Publication Data
Names: Holland, John, 1948-
Title: Responding to loss and bereavement in schools : a training resrouce to
assess, evaluate and improve the school response / John Holland.
Description: Philadelphia : Jessica Kingsley Publishers, 2016. | Includes
bibliographical references.
Identifiers: LCCN 2015032614 | ISBN 9781849056922 (alk. paper)
Subjects: LCSH: Loss (Psychology) in children. | Bereavement in children. |
Counseling.
Classification: LCC BF723.L68 H65 2016 | DDC 155.9/37083--dc23 LC record available at
http://lccn.loc.gov/2015032614

British Library Cataloguing in Publication Data
A CIP catalogue record for this book is available from the British Library

ISBN 978 1 84905 692 2
eISBN 978 1 78450 229 4

Printed and bound in the United States

To Susan, Rachel, Emma and Elizabeth

Acknowledgements

Thanks to my parents for their composure around death, Susan for her support and patience, and Beth Gower for her invaluable guidance in developing the project.

Contents

The initial responses to a death

The medium and longer-term responses to a death

About the Author

John Holland has been interested in bereavement, children, schools and education for several years and led the 'Lost for Words' project in Humberside, a loss-awareness project produced by educational psychologists and the Dove House Hospice in Hull.

John developed the 'Iceberg' project at the University of York, a doctoral study of the experiences of children and young people after parental death and the book *Understanding Children's Experiences of Parental Bereavement* (Holland 2001).

John is an associate fellow of the British Psychological Society employed in local government and his private practice.

Website: www.john-holland-ep.co.uk

Introduction

Responding to Loss and Bereavement in Schools helps you support pupils who have been bereaved or have experienced significant loss, and is based on the author's experience working with schools through training and research.

Although the focus of this book revolves around parental bereavement, the strategies can be adapted to any form of loss experienced in the school community.

For pupil support to be effective there must be awareness of the pupils' needs, and the power to make any changes. Power alone lacks direction and understanding of need; awareness alone lacks the ability to influence systems. The best outcomes are achieved by a combination of power, awareness and commitment of senior staff.

This book includes tools to develop support in the area of loss in schools. An audit of current practice uses a 'survey, analyse, plan and evaluate' cycle to help test the robustness of systems and identify 'bugs'. This is an active process, with evaluation of responses and modifications made.

The audit tool and questionnaire in Chapter 2 can identify gaps in knowledge and training, and these can be addressed though the exercises within the book, which provide basic training. It can help identify individuals with skills, experiences and interest, as well as raise awareness around the issue of loss and the need to respond and engage with pupils.

A swift 'light touch' intervention for pupils is preferable to the likely costly medium- or longer-term involvement of outside agencies. Speedy intervention safeguards pupils against the short-term effects of significant loss, increasing their chances of better life outcomes in the longer term. In terms of economics this makes sense in saving resources.

Research shows the long-term difficulties for some bereaved children, including reduced life chances if they disengage with education. Ribbens McCarthy and Jessop (2005) found some bereaved pupils withdrew from peers and others became involved in criminal behaviour; Cross (2005) found that bereaved children were at a greater risk of abuse.

For some pupils, parental death led to additional responsibilities at home, including child care and extra chores, and the dilution of childhood (Holland 2001). Bereaved children tend to leave home early, experience earlier sexual and partnering activities, and have parents who remarry. Teenage pregnancy, criminal or disruptive behaviours, depression and decline in self-esteem were all reported in the 'Iceberg' study.

'Iceberg' was a doctoral project at the University of York, carried out by the author into the effects of parental bereavement on children and described in *Understanding the Effects of Parental Bereavement* (Holland 2001), published by Jessica Kingsley Publishers.

Pupil behaviour may not be recognised as grieving and may increase the pupil's risk of exclusion and alienation from the school system if misinterpreted as wilful. School is a potential point of stability in children's lives and they and their families can be helped through this difficult period. Parental death is significant, and the effect on children and young people may be accentuated because of their lack of life experiences, control and understanding.

In the past, infant mortality was high and children gained understanding by involvement with death rites and first-hand observation of dying, through social learning theory (Bandura 1962). Today, adults may protect children, exclude them from involvement in the rites after death and deprive them of vicarious learning. Chadwick (2012) found that children may be 'shut out' of things, gathering half-truths and fantasies that are probably worse than the reality. At best this may only postpone children's grieving, leaving them confused and mistrustful of adults.

Parental bereavement is relatively frequent; Harrison and Harrington (2001) calculated that 2–6 per cent of children under 18 years of age are affected. Many schools have a pupil recently bereaved of a parent on roll, as did 35 per cent of North Yorkshire schools (Holland and McLennan 2015a); McGuinness (2009) found that 10 per cent of the adult workforce may be affected by a significant bereavement, and there may well be a similar level of bereaved staff in schools.

Bereavement is far from the only significant loss pupils may experience; other losses include parents' separation, divorce, re-partnering, imprisonment, illness, disability, moves of house and school, and the death of pets. A child being taken into public care has implications for them and their birth family and involves significant losses. Transitions affect all pupils as they move classes or schools, and the impact of all these changes may be underestimated by adults. The birth of a child, a young person leaving to go to university or a move of house may all have an impact to a greater or lesser degree and sometimes not as predicted.

Problems that can arise after loss
Family chaos

A significant loss or change causes disequilibrium within the family system until stability is restored. A major change in the family will be a significant event and they will take time to absorb the news. The family may initially be in a state of shock and overwhelmed. This period of instability may be sudden and problematic, and the family may need support, with new roles and changes implicitly or explicitly negotiated.

After a parental death, separation or loss, children may become 'clingy', concerned that the surviving parent may also die or leave, as they have become primed suddenly to the fragility of life. Peer group awareness and anxieties may be raised, and issues relating to previous losses may again surface.

The parenting team will have been halved by the death of the mother or father, and the surviving parent may work longer hours to support the family, and be less available to the children. Family members are normally a source of support and social learning, but after a death may not be emotionally available to the children, as they work through their own issues of loss.

Pupils who are 'looked after' may have experienced family chaos as well as moves of foster family, neighbourhood or area, and may have suffered physical or emotional harm as well as the loss of their birth family.

Tertiary losses

The death or separation of a parent is the presenting loss, and may be the only one recognised by many. There are potentially consequences that may flow indirectly from a death or parental separation. Further losses may take place whose ramifications and effect on the children are not so obvious. Loss is rarely simple and one-dimensional, and the effect of death may be complex, and more like a spider's web rather than a length of string. Unpredictable secondary losses may flow from the presenting loss, as ripples flow out when a stone is thrown into a pond, with implications over time and space. These tertiary effects may go unrecognised and include economic and social effects.

Economic consequences

There may be financial consequences after a death or separation, especially if the main earner has died or left home. The family may have a lower standard of living, which is accentuated if more child care is needed. The family may have to move house, perhaps even area. Life insurance cover may help to reduce the difficulties in the case of death.

If the family moves area, links in the local community will be lost. Children may lose contact with their familiar surroundings and support systems, such as friends, neighbours, school, doctors, clubs, organisations and church. Children may already feel isolated and different after the death, but more so if their new peers have a different accent or language. The death of a parent or carer is less common than separation although this may have similar consequences, such as children losing contact with a parent, moving house or school and having step-parents.

Psychological issues

Change and loss are lifelong human experiences and it is only when they are overwhelming that there may be problems. Babies are aware of separation from carers, and research by Bowlby (1963, 1981) showed the importance of secure attachment bonds and effects of loss. Children experiencing significant loss may be left with memories. The adults the child encounters may be oblivious to their background, so although the adults are aware of emotional markers, such as adverse behaviour or learning, they may not link these to the context of the young person's experiences.

Children's cognitive and emotional responses may not be synchronised after a significant loss. Their cognitive, higher-level functioning may be out of synch with their more primitive emotional reactions. This needs to be borne in mind as anger or withdrawal may be signs of grieving but misunderstood by adults. A pupil showing signs of anger and disruption may be seen simply as a 'naughty' rather than a 'needy' child. A quiet pupil may be sad and feeling emotionally low and drained, but staff may not be alerted to their needs as they are not a problem in class.

The Vygotskian approach (Vygotsky 1978) is to find the pupil's level of understanding and to plan an intervention accordingly, not pitching things as too complex or too simple but 'just right'. The level of understanding needs to be gained to enable work to be carried out in their 'zone of proximal development' (Chaiklin 2003). If this approach is not used, the pupil may feel patronised with too simple assumptions, or feel lost with too complex ones. Children need to understand and it is a challenge to pitch explanations at the right level.

THEORIES OF GRIEVING

Theories of grieving are relatively recent. Kubler-Ross (1980) suggested that the bereaved went through emotional stages, such as shock, denial, anger and resolution, which tended to be thought of as lasting around two years. This can be seen as deterministic, as well as pathologising grief, and is extrapolated from research with adults.

Mallon's (1997) division of children's grieving into three phases of protest, disorganisation and re-organisation is useful, as is Fox's (1985) suggestion that children have four tasks after a death: 'understanding', 'grieving', 'commemorating', and 'going on'. This is helpful to frame the needs of children in terms of adults responding to their needs, and links with the thoughts of many of those who took part in 'Iceberg'.

Stroebe and Schut (1999) proposed a dual processing model in which the bereaved oscillate between grieving and restorative work, which perhaps explains why children seem to be sad, then moments later are playing as if nothing has happened. Children are likely to be processing what has happened but need 'time out' from potentially overwhelming loss. Goldman (1996) thought that bereaved children may be caught in 'frozen blocks of time' and need adult support to help them.

Children will learn vicariously through observations (Bandura 1962), and they may lack the encounters and involvement with death compared with children's experiences in our relatively recent past.

CHILDREN'S UNDERSTANDING OF DEATH

It can be difficult for adults to know what children and young people understand about death. This question was addressed in the 'Iceberg' project. The results give guidance rather than being definitive, and the best way of finding out what children understand is to ask them and gauge their understanding from their responses.

Until around two years old, children will have the notion of separation from an attachment figure rather than the concept of death. Somebody whom they are attached to is no longer there and this may cause distress. From around the age of two children will be developing their language but tend to think in literal terms and have confusing ideas about death. They may wonder about the physical wellbeing of the deceased person, such as how they eat and go to the toilet. They may know the word 'death' but not understand it fully or think that it applies to them.

Chadwick (2012) quotes a four-year-old child dying in a hospice as saying that he knew what happens after you die – 'Sister flushes you down the toilet' – based on what happened to his tropical fish!

Between the ages of four and eight years old, children develop intellectually and emotionally, and gradually become more aware that death has a cause, cannot be reversed and may happen to anyone. Their language develops and their cognitive understanding is greater, but they may still be literal in their thinking. Children may have fantasies far worse than the reality if not given the facts by adults who are trying to protect them.

Children may have 'magical thinking' and feel responsible for the death, believing that their destructive fantasies, such as wishing someone dead, have come true. They may feel that the death is a form of punishment to them for doing something wrong.

From about eight years of age onwards, most children are developing an adult understanding of death but there may still be signs of magical thinking and confusion. Their own future death gradually becomes more of a reality. During the adolescent stage, young people's concept of death becomes more abstract and they understand more of the consequences and issues involved. It is important to consider children's level of understanding in relation to their age and respond accordingly.

Children's understanding of death	
Age of child	Understanding of death
0–4 years	Emergent
4–8 years	Limited
8–16 years	Fuller

The table above is only a rough guide, as some children will gain a fuller understanding earlier, others later, depending on their cognitive ability and experience. Children with language difficulties or those who are on the autism spectrum and take things more literally may take longer to develop an abstract understanding.

It is helpful to use the correct language with children, such as the word 'death' rather than euphemisms such as 'loss'. Children will find this less confusing, and can 'grow into' the word and build on it with experience. The word 'death' per se does not have the same connotations for young children as it does for adults.

It is likely that children will have a similar level of understanding in relation to the other losses that they may encounter, such as their parents separating or divorcing, having a parent in prison or being in the care system. The Vygotskian notion of finding what children understand about the loss and responding accordingly seems a sensible strategy where children have experienced significant loss. Blackburn (1991) found a mismatch between bereaved children's understanding of death and what their teachers thought they knew.

In Wordsworth's 1798 poem 'We are Seven' (Till 1994), the eight-year-old has a very clear idea of death! This would have probably been similar for children in our relatively recent past, as death was encountered more with a high level of infant mortality.

Religious and cultural issues

The religions of the West – Christianity, Islam and Judaism – have their roots in the Abrahamic traditions of the Middle-East. The Eastern religions include Buddhism, Hinduism, Sikhism, Confucianism and Taoism.

It is impossible to generalise about the post-death religious practices, rites and customs, although the Western religions of Judaism, Christianity and Islam generally differ from the Eastern religions in terms of treatment of the body. With Islam and Judaism the body is generally buried quickly; cremation has become more common recently in Christianity although there is generally not the same speed of burial. The Eastern religions have different rites and rituals including cremation on pyres, sky burials, and the scattering of ashes on the Ganges.

Religions are not homogenous and there are divisions within them. An example is the broad division within Christianity between Catholic, Orthodox and Protestant, but there are other subdivisions including Methodists, Baptists and Quakers.

The area of religion and post-death rites is one where offence can easily be unintentionally given and good connections with local religious and community leaders will help to avoid pitfalls, especially as communities are becoming more diverse.

Creating links and communicating with leaders will help you to gain a better understanding of the customs, rites and responsibilities after death. Children will naturally assume that what happens in their home and community is the norm and may be both interested and confused when they encounter other practices.

How to use *Responding to Loss and Bereavement in Schools*: Menu of suggested action

Before beginning analysis or training it is important to gain an overview of the area of pupil bereavement and loss by reading the first part of *Responding to Loss and Bereavement in Schools*, that is, 'The Role of the School'. For greater insights into the experiences of children after the death of a parent you could read *Understanding Children's Experiences of Parental Bereavement* (Holland 2001), based on the doctoral research project 'Iceberg' into the experiences of children after the death of a parent.

Next, critically examine what is currently in place at school, completing the survey of current responses, testing any policy in place and assessing the skill levels of staff. This will help identify any training needed and individuals who could carry out a role. Staff training can then be tailored appropriately.

The topics and exercises can be used for training and to stimulate discussion. The exercises are best delivered in a group, with a facilitator leading with appropriate questions and challenges. Interactive group sessions can help to engage the participants and may be more productive than a purely formal didactic or PowerPoint approach.

Summaries and flipcharts may help visual learners as well as providing reminders to reinforce learning points. *Responding to Loss and Bereavement in Schools* is underpinned by research through projects such as 'Iceberg' and how the needs of children and young people can be met.

CHAPTER 1

The Role of the School

Introduction

Pupils spend significant time at school, which could play a key supporting role for them and their family after a death or other significant loss, and they may contact you for advice.

Holland (1993) identified a 'training gap' in Humberside schools. Schools rated bereavement an important area, but lacked the skills to respond effectively. Lowton and Higginson (2003) found that staff in schools were concerned about doing the 'right thing'; this was echoed in Holland's (2001) findings that teachers wanted to help but were unsure as to how and were wary of causing an upset.

Dyregrov (1991) considered schools well placed to offer support, with knowledge of their pupils and families, and the local religious and cultural context (Oyebode and Owens 2013). Tracey's (2006) study of bereaved daughters showed the positive role that teachers can play after bereavement. Berg *et al.* (2014) stressed the importance of school-based support to help to support school performance The research was a large Swedish study of children experiencing parental death before 15 years of age, comparing their academic results when 15 to 16 years old. Parental death was associated with lower academic grades.

In the 'Iceberg' project, the bereaved pupils themselves thought that schools could have offered better support but that they lacked the knowledge and understanding to help. 'Iceberg' pupils thought that relatively simple strategies, such as acknowledging their loss and allowing time and space for listening, would have helped.

Schools are embedded in the community and Bronfenbrenner's model (1979, 1997) helps frame them as well positioned to support pupils. In Bronfenbrenner's model, the pupil is located in the bull's eye of a series of concentric circles. Parents, carers and the immediate family are in the inner circle, potentially able to offer significant support. The family may in theory be a key support for bereaved pupils, but if things are chaotic after the death they may be struggling with their own grief and unable to support the children.

The next outer concentric circle comprises the neighbourhood, school, community organisations, social, religious or leisure groups and clubs such as the scouts or youth groups. The family may have a wider network of outer family and friends and the children may have their own network of contacts.

Local and central government are located in the outer circles, as is the cultural context – all potentially sources of support. There are bi-directional effects between the elements in the model: the grief of a pupil may both affect and be affected by others. Looking at Bronfenbrenner's model in a different way, the concentric circles could be used to map out emotional closeness. Relations may not live within the geographical area but be linked through emotional closeness and be closer to the bull's eye than the geography would suggest.

All these potential points of support can be seen as blocks, placed to help at a time of crisis. The effects of the blocks may be positive, neutral or negative, depending on how well they are mobilised. Barriers to supporting children include ineffective communication and engagement difficulties, such as failing to understand their needs, or not interacting for fear of causing an upset. School could help to engage and mobilise these positive blocks of support by suggesting them to the family as well as making contacts to help to activate the blocks.

Families and children may become isolated if others are reluctant to engage with them, and this may be difficult if the potential supporters do not know how to approach the family. The more positive blocks of support that are mobilised, the more likely it is that there will be a better outcome for the children.

Schools are in a potentially positive position as they lack emotional closeness and may not be caught up within the family chaos and inertia. A good relationship with families underpins the effectiveness of the response, making it easier for schools to offer support and guidance, and to gain consents for sharing information. Schools may also be able to help pupils and family engage with the general community and neighbourhood support. Careful thought needs to be given as to how to activate the potential blocks of support.

If school is not involved in supporting the pupil, these blocks of help will be lost to the family. Whether schools and staff recognise this potential and perceive themselves in this role will depend on their level of understanding, experience, awareness, skills and training.

The importance of planning and policy

Schools are a potential block of support for pupils and families. Planning is a key part of the bereavement response, and having a system in place before any loss will ensure that things can be considered during a time of calm. If a plan is not in place, the response will be ad-hoc and have to be re-thought each time. Things may more easily be missed or forgotten at a time of crisis if a plan has not been considered in advance.

Schools in the UK tend not to have a policy in place. This is in contrast with countries such as Australia or Denmark. In a study comparing Australian and English secondary schools, 15 per cent of English schools had a policy, compared with 94 per cent of Australian schools (Rowlings and Holland 2000). In the case of North Yorkshire schools, 35 per cent had a policy in place (Holland and McLeannan 2015a), as did 39 per cent of Hull schools and 23 per cent of North Suffolk schools (Holland and Wilkinson 2015b).

There is a view that as all deaths are different, an 'ad-hoc' response is appropriate, as found by Tracey and Holland (2008). There are patterns that are common in all deaths, including how to respond to the pupil, the family and the school community. If there is no plan, then each bereavement or loss has to be planned from scratch without the benefit of the experience of previous ones. A plan does not have to be set in stone, but forms a basis of core ideas for the initial response and can be flexible to adapt to circumstances, with changes used to feed back into revisions for the next time.

Questions to consider when planning a policy or procedure include:

- What to do if school is unsure of the facts: how will they be clarified and by whom?

- Who should contact the family, and how: by telephone, letter or visit?

- How could the school respond to the family? Should flowers, a wreath, a letter or a card be sent?

- What information is needed from the family about the death?

- What happens if a bereaved pupil is in school when the news is received?

- Who should go on a home visit?

- What questions and advice could the family ask you about?

- How long should pupils be away from school after a death?

- What is the date of the funeral? Will the school be represented and by whom?

- Should advice be given about children attending the funeral?

- Are there any religious or community implications and if so, who are the relevant local religious or community leaders?

- Which agencies and neighbourhood organisations could be mobilised to support the family?

- If the media are interested, who liaises with them, and is local authority support needed?

- Who needs to know about the death at school and how will they be told?

- Will consent or agreement be sought from the family to inform the school community, and what if this is not given?

- How are questions from staff, other parents, pupils or the community answered, and who responds to them?

- How is contact to be maintained with the family and by whom?

- How can other children who could potentially be emotionally affected by the death of a peer's parent be identified, such as close friends of the bereaved pupil?

- What mechanism is needed to advise supply staff or staff absent on courses or through illness?

- What are the implications for absent pupils?

- How can the bereaved pupil's initial transition back to school be planned then how can they be monitored over the long term?

- Can the school manage the bereavement on its own? Does it need to seek outside support and, if so, from where?

- How can anniversaries and important dates be identified and managed at school, including anniversaries of the death, birthdays and father's and mother's days?

- How can information be identified and passed between classes and schools?

- When will the policy be reviewed and who will be responsible for this action?

Having a school policy means making best guesses at situations that may arise and anticipating how to respond. Any policy may not meet all the circumstances that arise, but if it has been carefully thought through and tested, then it is hoped it will be fit for purpose.

The source of the news of the death needs to be considered. It may arrive directly from the family through a telephone call or a visit. However, if the news arrives indirectly through the 'grapevine' or from a family friend or neighbour, consideration needs to be given as to how to tactfully verify the news with the family. The news may even arrive through the media, television or radio, and thought needs to be given as to how to respond.

The family could be responded to by returning the telephone call and arranging a home visit or whatever is considered appropriate. It may be difficult to discuss sensitive issues over the phone and a brief call followed by a visit when convenient for the family could be an option.

If the family is to be visited at home, a decision needs to be made as to who is to visit and whether, especially on the first occasion, one or two staff should attend. There are advantages in two people visiting, if only to keep children amused and be an extra pair of eyes and ears.

Before making a visit or a telephone call, take care to consider what information is needed from the family as well as what questions they may ask. Things to ask could include clarification as to what has happened, what the children have been told and agreement as to how much information to disclose to staff and pupils. Information and rumours may already be circulating in the community and it may not be realistic to hide this from pupils.

The family may ask about the effect on the children and how long they should stay away from school.

Another consideration is what to do if a pupil is in school when news of the death arrives. The pupil needs to hear the news from their family, but what if this is not possible in the short term? This may not become an issue unless news of the death becomes known to other pupils at the school. In this case contingencies need to be made to keep the pupil safe.

With regard to responding to the family, this could be by sending flowers, a letter or a card, or a combination of these. It is helpful to know the date and location of the funeral, who should attend and whether flowers or a wreath are to be sent. The family's wishes need to be paramount here and they may request donations for an appropriate charity. The family may ask about whether the children should attend the funeral. The general rule is to give children the choice but prepare them with explanations and include a visit to the church and/or crematorium.

Keeping in touch with the family may be helpful, and a particular member of staff could carry out this task.

It is useful to consider any potential religious or cultural implications and, if necessary, to seek advice from community and religious leaders. There may also be neighbourhood or local community organisations that could be mobilised to support the family. Ideally, contacts are established before a death occurs.

Media involvement may make things difficult, especially if the media are camped outside the home or the school. A member of staff could act as the media liaison person and deal with radio or television crews. The local authority may have an appropriate department that can help and provide advice.

A system of communication to pass on information needs to be developed. This could be through staff briefings or personal contacts, depending on the size of the school. Those away on leave, on a course or sick, as well as supply staff, need to be considered, as do staff such as teaching assistants, office staff, road-crossing people, lunch-time supervisors and those running early morning or after-school clubs.

Thought needs to be given to how and what to tell other pupils. This depends on their age and closeness to the bereaved child. Young children may be best told in their classes by their teacher; older pupils and those not close to the bereaved pupil could be told in lager groups, such as at an assembly.

It may be difficult to know what words to use. The form of words is best rehearsed and could be along the lines of 'I have got some very sad news...' Things should be explained factually, bearing in mind the age of pupils.

Be prepared for staff and pupils to ask questions. It is likely that the news will cause distress to some children, and staff should be on hand to help with a supply of tissues. The pupils themselves may want to respond, and suggestions need to be considered and responded to with tact.

Thought needs to be given to identifying pupils who may be emotionally affected by the death, including friends of the bereaved pupil, and consideration also needs to be given to absent pupils. In some circumstances it may be appropriate to send a letter home to all pupils to clarify the school's response.

The bereaved pupil's return to school needs to be carefully planned with the family, with consideration given to a gradual transition, sensitive acknowledgement of the bereavement and support offered.

Pupils need to be monitored over time, especially at significant events such as the anniversary of the death, birthdays or times of celebration. This may be best achieved by the class teacher or mentor but should not be left to chance. A system needs to be in place to pass information on when pupils change class and especially school, to ensure awareness.

The policy needs to be relevant to the context of your school. Not everybody needs to be involved in developing the policy, but all could contribute to feedback on the draft plans, and contribute to an evaluation after a death. It is important that all are aware of the policy and pathways. For the bereavement response to be as effective as possible, all staff need to be aware of how loss can affect pupils, and those staff working on interventions with bereaved children may need more training.

TENDER MOMENTS

Having a policy and procedure in place is part of an effective response but they need to be explicitly clear to all.

Once I was in a tender transporting from shore to ship. The crew knew the procedure for disembarking but did not tell the passengers. Most passengers stood up to disembark, and the boat began to rock, until the crew directed each section to disembark in order, according to the procedure!

Potential roles in schools

There will be a range of individuals in schools with variation in their experiences, interests, capacities, empathy, understanding and training about bereavement. It is important to include governors, as they may be able to make a positive contribution in mobilising the community and supporting staff.

Not all staff may be comfortable with the area of death. Individuals have different experiences of life, and a significant death may prime them to have empathy and understanding of a bereaved pupil. In contrast, personal experience may overwhelm and prevent them from engaging with bereaved pupils.

Staff in schools can become involved in different roles in regard to loss and bereavement. Potential roles at school are 'champions', 'strategists', 'interventionists' and 'interactionists'. By naming a role relating to a function it breaks down a large area into manageable chunks, with each role suiting different people's interests and experiences. No one person needs to take on everything, although it is assumed that all will at least be interactionists; each role has different training needs, which can be addressed through the exercises in this book.

Champions

Champions are those having a special interest in the area of loss and bereavement and able to promote it in school. They may have had their awareness raised by experience of loss and bereavement. Champions are key to promoting the area by helping to raise awareness generally and by developing training, policies and procedures. They may facilitate in a wider sense rather than deal with the finer points.

Strategists

Strategists are those in a position of power in school who are able to promote structures. Their role is to develop effective systems and ensure that these are laid down in policies and procedures. These need to include the Key or Golden Moments, explained later in the book – crucial points that need to be carefully managed. Strategists will need an interest in and awareness of the area of bereavement and be able to analyse what is needed at the systems level.

Interventionists

Interventionists offer additional support that children may need beyond what is generally provided. They need to be able to respond to and help pupils in greater depth. They should be able to carry out interventions with the bereaved pupil such as listening, finding out information for them, or running peer support groups in school.

Interventionists need a good knowledge of the implications of bereavement for pupils and the ability to support interventions when needed. For this they require more detailed training than generalists (those who do not have one of the four major roles outlined here).

Interactionists

Interactionists are all those in school who may encounter a bereaved pupil, and include teachers and ancillary workers. Interactionists need to be aware of pupil needs after a death or significant loss, and to have a basic understanding of loss. Interactionists need to be confident in their ability to respond to pupils, such as acknowledging their loss. They need an awareness of the potential issues for pupils, including learning and behaviour, and to be aware of the potentially far-reaching effects of loss. They need to understand that the bereaved child may feel isolated, different and even embarrassed, and needs time to adjust to their new circumstances.

Training needs vary across staff in terms of their potential roles, although all would benefit from basic loss-awareness training.

Adults do not need to be counsellors to respond to bereaved pupils; however, they need to understand how bereaved pupils can be helped and the importance of acknowledging loss and have the notion of an appropriate response. Most pupils will not need counselling after a loss, but would benefit from counselling-like skills, such as empathetic and active listening – basically a human and humane approach.

The importance of information gathering and communication

Communication is crucial from the outset when news of the death is received. This includes identifying what information is needed, and how it can be gained and distributed to where it is needed. Clear links need to be thought through and established – each link is crucial to the process.

It is important to have a clear idea of the facts about the death in order to judge what response is needed. Good communications need to be established with the family, not only to offer help and support but to have an agreed clear strategy about matters such as telling the news to the school community, knowing what the bereaved pupil has been told and arranging the pupil's return to school.

There are dangers in divulging information without discussing it with the family as they may regard some things as confidential. Communications within school need to be considered, such as what and how to tell staff and pupils. Channels of communication need to be developed in the policy and tested to ensure that messages and information reach those who need them – office and auxiliary staff, in particular, need to be kept in the loop.

Language needs to be clear and unambiguous, and staff should feel able to seek clarification if they do not fully understand the message. Communication channels need to be maintained with the family, to monitor and check if they need support and to quickly clarify issues raised by the bereaved pupil.

Children may ask difficult questions, such as where the dead person has gone or why and how they died. Care must be taken not to conflict with what the family has told them. Communication with children and young people needs to at the appropriate level, bearing in mind their development and cognitive stage. It is important to check that the information has been understood by the pupil, using strategies such as asking them to explain back in their own words.

Even language that superficially seems clear may not be understood by children. There may be a language information gap. If children are told that somebody has died from a heart attack, they may be puzzled as to how a heart can be 'attacked' and a better explanation may be that the heart has worn out. Children may not understand the information given or misunderstand without realising, and adults may make the same mistake.

Much communication is non-verbal and adults need to consider their body language when interacting with the family and pupils. It needs to be 'open', not 'closed', to encourage engagement. Body posture and eye contact must be considered so as not to discourage pupils from talking. Silences should not be seen as difficult or as a reluctance to engage; although they may be difficult for the adult, they may be helpful to the pupil.

The Key or Golden Moments

Project 'Iceberg' identified four Key or Golden Moments for children and young people after the death of a parent. These are crucial times where responses are needed to help to provide effective support and minimise the chance of pupils being alienated from school.

The first Golden Moment is when news of the death arrives in school. The second is the period before the funeral. The third is on the pupil's return to school. The fourth is when the pupil changes school. These Key Moments may go unrecognised by adults and pupils alike.

School has the potential to provide support, influence and guidance at these key points, and having an effective continuing relationship with the family will help.

Golden Moment 1: Receiving news of the death

The first Golden Moment is when news of the death breaks in school. The school may be contacted by the family, or the news may be received through another source. The initial response is to make contact with the family to clarify what has happened.

The initial contact may set the tone for the relationship and affect future interactions with the pupil and their family. It helps if there is a good relationship with the family and they have a positive view of the school.

Initial contact could be made by telephone with a follow-up meeting with the family where offers of advice and help can be given. A written response by card, letter or flowers could be considered. The early proactive support may be a 'light touch', but it may well impact positively on the family and pupils. In the Bronfenbrenner model (Bronfenbrenner 1979, 1997) the pupil is central, but within a network of relationships at different levels.

Thought needs to be given as to what to say when visiting or making a telephone call; you need to predict and rehearse questions that you may be asked and those you need to ask. Saying something is far better than saying nothing, as words can always be rephrased if they come out wrongly. Where nothing is said, the situation may be harder to retrieve, especially as the mind-set of the bereaved may assume a lack of interest and care.

If planned conversations do not follow the predicted pathway, at least you have a plan in place, though it is important to be flexible and respond to the needs of the family and children.

All this is easier if a policy and procedure are in place in terms of protocols, including who is to contact the family, the methods of contact and responding to the funeral.

The role of the person making the initial contact depends on the context. The head teacher could make the initial contact and visit with another member of staff who could then take the role of liaising with the family. Having two staff members attending initially may seem to be swamping the family, but it may be the better option as things are less likely to be forgotten. Extreme tact and empathy are clearly needed on the first visit, with condolences offered; the initial visit could also focus on establishing the facts and offering help.

There may be media attention, especially with a high-profile death. The media may approach school for information, which should be resisted without family agreement.

It is helpful if the facts are clarified and also what the children have been told. It is worth mentioning that it is impossible to 'contain' information in a community and indeed within a family, as information will 'leak' out. If children are not told the truth, they will hear pieces of information that may or may not be correct. It is preferable to tell children what is happening in terms that they can understand rather than insulate them from information. Their fears and fantasies may exceed what has actually happened. The family could be guided to be honest with the children, while using appropriate language and avoiding euphemisms, jargon and complex medical terms.

Families may seek advice about their children's understanding and how to help them, and whether the children should attend the funeral. The date of the funeral could be clarified – the second Golden Moment – and the family helped in terms of seeking support in the neighbourhood through their own and the school's contacts. Local informal and formal networks may be able to offer support, including organisations such as church or social clubs. The family may also have their own ideas but need help to facilitate contacts.

A dialogue needs to be established about the pupil's return to school – the third Golden Moment – and how this crucial transition will be managed.

Care needs to be taken with a letter of condolence. It is probably a good strategy to make this short and to the point, with an offer of help. For example:

> Dear Mr Brown,
>
> We were all very sorry to hear about the death of your wife, and the school community extends our sympathy and condolences at this difficult time.
>
> I will telephone you shortly to see if we can help, and in the meantime do not hesitate to contact me if we can help in any way.
>
> Yours sincerely,
>
> Head Teacher

The formality and tone will depend on the circumstances and your relationship with the family. In a similar way, any telephone conversation initially needs to express condolences and ask the family if it is a convenient time to talk; if it is not, then arrange a convenient time to phone back.

Golden Moment 2: The funeral

The funeral is a public acknowledgement of the death, a public rite of passage as well as a legal method of dealing hygienically with a body. The second Golden Moment relates to the period before the funeral. The funeral usually takes place shortly after death, although the context and provisions vary with religion and culture. There are differences in aspects of bereavement and the expected grieving response, which may be subdued, an open expression of grief or a celebration of the deceased's life.

There are cultural and social differences in the laying out and viewing of the body, even within religious groups, and cremation is not always the custom. The involvement of women and children may vary within religions. There is a wide variation in religious beliefs as to what happens after death and the belief or otherwise of an afterlife.

The funeral is a family event, a rite of passage like a wedding or christening; it is also a public event, providing an opportunity for the wider community to pay their respects. Project 'Iceberg' found that many children did not attend the funeral. Some were distracted by being sent away on a day trip on the day of the funeral. Others were simply denied access, and for many of them there were long-term implications (Holland 2004). Many children felt anger and regret years later, as well as raising issues about adult trust. The children not attending often felt excluded from the family at a very significant event. The research showed that it was not attending the funeral that was important but whether children had an informed choice as to whether to attend or not.

Children benefit from preparation as to what happens, and could be shown the church and crematorium before the funeral. This needs to be arranged when no funerals are taking place and the proceedings can be explained. The sight of the coffin carried in and the procedures will then not come as a complete surprise. Explanations relating to the order of the service and how adults behave should help to prepare and reassure children. Without explanations children may construct myths about what happens, such as the coffin being burnt in view at a crematorium, and they may see a funeral as being a 'scary' event.

There is a danger of putting an adult construction on funerals. Children attending a funeral will take what they can from the event in terms of their understanding of death, and will see it as a family event. In retrospect, when asked how they felt about attending a funeral, none of the 'Iceberg' children regarded it with the horror that adults perhaps anticipate. Memories focused on the 'getting together' and family party element of the funeral, and older children felt pride in seeing the people attending and paying respects to their parent.

The results relating to attending the chapel of rest were similar, although the experience was not positive for a small group of younger girls. Preparation and choice again seem important, and children should not be forced to attend against their will. There are advantages in children seeing that the person is actually dead rather than the potential of fearing that they may be buried alive, as in horror movies.

Since 'Iceberg' established the importance of children being given the choice about attending the funeral of a parent, this can be used as advice for the family. Once the funeral has taken place, the opportunity has obviously passed.

Golden Moment 3: The return to school

The third Golden Moment is on the pupil's return to school, and this needs to be carefully planned. Some pupils may return shortly after the death, others may not return immediately and be away for some time. Continued liaison with the family will ensure that the school can provide advice and guidance.

This can be a difficult time if children are reluctant to return, and sometimes parents may want them to stay off school. Parents may use children for support and they in turn may wish to remain at home to be involved in the comings and goings of visitors and family. Children may want to stay at home if they are concerned that the remaining parent may also die.

In the 'Iceberg' research, many children felt isolated and welcomed even just a brief acknowledgment of their bereavement on their return to school, with an offer to listen to them if needed. Adults should not be afraid of reaching out to a bereaved pupil and making the first move to begin a conversation, but they should avoid pressing the matter. If nothing is said, then the pupil may think that the death is not known about or that the adults do not care.

Care must be taken not to overwhelm pupils with acknowledgements, but individuals may be able to choose an appropriate opportunity. Staff with close relationships with the pupil, such as their class or tutor group teacher, are ideally placed to offer them time to discuss the bereavement.

It is important to initially acknowledge the death. If you are unsure as to what to say to a bereaved pupil, then keep it simple, such as saying that you are sorry to hear about the death, and leave it open for them to talk at the time or later if they need to.

Ideas for engaging with pupils include:

- It is better to say something than nothing to a bereaved pupil. If the words come out in a clumsy way, you can refine the comment. If you say nothing, that may give a message to the bereaved that you either do not know or care about the death.

- Do not hijack the conversation and talk about your experiences, such as when your old Aunt Maud died. Relating your own experiences to the pupil is not helpful unless you are specifically asked.

- Saying 'I know how you feel' is not helpful, as nobody can really know how another individual feels.

- Listening is better than talking!

- Silences can be golden. There is no need to fill space with talking if being quiet is helpful to the pupil.

- Do not to use platitudes as they devalue the experiences of the bereaved.

- Do not positively reframe the death. If the bereaved positively reframes the death, then consider agreeing or saying nothing; but it is not helpful for you to initiate this.

- It is not a good idea to hint that somebody could have done something different, such as calling an ambulance earlier.

- If you cannot make time immediately to speak with a pupil wishing to talk, then arrange to meet them as soon as possible afterwards.

- If a bereaved pupil wants to talk about their experiences, do not change the subject.

- Communicate with children in a child-friendly way and not as adult to adult. Simplify complex language and do not assume children have an adult-like understanding of death. Check pupils' understanding if necessary.

- If staff do not think that children need a response, then the subject may become the 'elephant in the classroom', as bereaved pupils are unlikely to raise the subject themselves if they do not anticipate a positive response.

- Be careful with body language and non-verbal communication, especially if you are uncomfortable with the subject. Awkward or negative body language may deter pupils from asking for help.

- Remember that 'Iceberg' children were very positive about those staff who made an effort to engage with them.

There is a danger of social isolation for pupils if staff and peers do not know what to say to them. This isolation may lead to the pupil becoming withdrawn, aggressive or feeling alienated from school, with the potential for truancy and involvement in antisocial activities.

Many in the 'Iceberg' study felt very isolated on their return to school. Few felt able to approach staff for help or considered that the school had helped prepare them for the bereavement in cases where the death was expected. Sadly, a minority of pupils thought that being ignored was helpful as their family was in emotional chaos and school was a place of calm and refuge.

Some children in 'Iceberg' lacked information, understanding, control, acknowledgement and facilitation after bereavement and felt that the school could have helped them by just listening and providing explanations about things that they did not understand. Explanations should only be given after checking with the family.

There was a view from a number of 'Iceberg' subjects that school could have helped by telling their peers about the death. This is problematic without liaising with the family, underlining the importance of a good home–school relationship.

In the medium and longer term, key dates should be recorded and regular contact kept between the family and school. New staff will need to be told as appropriate, and details also passed on whenever there is a change of class or school.

Some in 'Iceberg' thought that 'death education' would have helped them to be better prepared for the bereavement. Both Purdy (2013) and Goldman (2014) found that schools can potentially help support children proactively through their losses through appropriate education.

Staff with a special interest in the area of loss and bereavement may be able to offer interventions to bereaved children. Essentially, this will be to provide a listening ear and help the pupil's understanding, with the agreement of the family.

There are other strategies that can be used to help bereaved children and encourage them to talk about anything that troubles them. Activities such as playing games may help if pupils are able to relax and feel that things are less focused on them.

Some children may like to use puppet play, while others prefer to express their feelings by drawing or painting. Pupils could then be asked to explain their artwork, giving them an opportunity to talk about how they are feeling.

Older children may be able to express their thoughts in writing or other avenues such as free play, role play and drama activities.

Group activities can sometimes help, as hearing the views of peers may reassure bereaved pupils that their feelings and thoughts are 'normal'. Loss groups could include pupils having experienced a variety of losses. This will depend on how comfortable and confident pupils are about working in such a group, and whether such groups are generally run in school.

Circle time can be used to help pupils, as they can self-monitor and choose what they wish to share. This potentially gives them a forum, although for some this may be too public, in which case a question box could be used for them to post notes about what is concerning them. Children may be helped by keeping memory boxes, with mementos of special memories, or a book of photographs or drawings.

Children need reassurance that being upset or tearful is a natural response to grief. It is not sensible to make over-compensatory allowances for bereaved pupils as they still need structure in their life and at school. If there are behavioural difficulties in school, then pupils could be taken aside afterwards to discuss how and why things went wrong and additionally to ask how they are feeling in relation to the bereavement. Pupils could be given a safe place in the classroom or allowed to leave quietly, if they wish, if their emotions are raw.

Pupils are helped by adults being open with them, giving them honest answers to questions, listening to their stories, explaining things with great care and seeking information if they do not know the answer. It is important to keep any promises made and to maintain contact with the family to check if they need support and to keep them informed of how the pupil is doing by monitoring their progress.

The period of grieving should not be underestimated, and pupils need monitoring over time and around special occasions such as anniversaries of the death or on birthdays and other special times, including at Christmas.

The return to school is a Golden Moment, although pupils need to be monitored in the short, medium and longer term, in relation to learning and their emotional wellbeing.

Golden Moment 4: Change of class or school

The fourth Key Moment is the pupil's transfer to another class, or school, either through an anticipated move, such as from primary school to secondary school or an unplanned change if the family moves house or area.

If school has monitored the pupil after the bereavement, then this valuable information can be quickly passed on to the new school. If records are not passed on, there is the danger that adverse behaviour or issues with learning may not be seen in the context of the bereavement, and the pupil will be perceived as being 'naughty' rather than 'needy'. If seen as 'naughty', the pupil may not have their needs met and may not receive a humane approach, and could be in danger of becoming alienated from school.

Evaluation

An evaluation and feedback loop in the policy is important as it helps it to evolve over time and to avoid inertia developing by responding to change. 'Top-down' and 'bottom-up' changes can both be effective through the feedback loop, given coordination between those with the power and those with the knowledge. The 'top-down' element can help to develop a coordinated system, while 'bottom-up' changes from those engaging with the bereaved pupil can be crucial in identifying and analysing unmet needs or circumstance and providing feedback to modify the systems and interventions.

An evaluation could take place after each significant loss to determine what went well and what went not so well; and after a time for reflection the family and pupil could be asked for their feedback.

When disaster strikes

Responding to Loss and Bereavement in Schools is intended to help schools to be self-sufficient in relation to significant loss within the school community and to alert you to your potential outside support.

Occasionally a loss or death may occur in traumatic circumstances, such as a pupil killed in an accident, which is witnessed by other pupils. An event like this may potentially overwhelm the school, and immediate specialist critical incident debriefing may be needed for those involved, although the other responses to the loss will still be necessary.

The exercises in Part 3 are also still relevant, but you may need to seek ongoing outside specialist support for the family, the pupils who are directly affected and even the wider school community. The involvement of the media may also make things more complex.

All the procedures and policies in place will be needed and relevant, and your plan could include where to seek outside support in such circumstances. The local authority through educational psychologists and social workers may be able to offer direct support and also may be able to help in relation to the media. Medical services may be able to offer support through clinical psychologists and specialist nurses. Plans or procedures need to consider this aspect and you need to have built up a list of potential contacts, ideally having made contact with and spoken to these potential helpers.

CHAPTER 2

The Audit

You need to go through a process of 'survey, analyse and plan' to audit what is in place in school. This provides an opportunity to reflect on the current provision, or if there is no policy or provision, to provide guidance for developing a proactive approach. Staff strengths and training needs can also be determined. The exercises provide an opportunity to air the subject, share thoughts and begin to address training needs.

The first section relates to questions that need to be addressed. The answers will begin the process of resolving any gaps in provision, including what happens after a significant loss.

The school audit

Questions to help the school identify what is in place and the strengths and gaps

Do you have a policy in place in relation to pupil bereavement?

Briefly outline the policy or procedure.

What provision is currently in place at school to respond to pupils who have experienced bereavement?

Would you describe your approach to bereavement as proactive or reactive? Is your response related to a plan or policy currently in place, or is it reactive in relation to the perceived need at the time?

Outline if the response is a hybrid of both approaches.

Who is in charge of the area of loss and bereavement?

Describe the pathway taken from the news of the death of a pupil's parent until the process ends.

What training do staff at school have, if any?

What support links do you have with outside agencies?

After a death do you liaise with the family?

If so, who is involved, and how and when precisely does this happen?

How is the return of pupils to school after bereavement monitored?

Are pupils monitored over the medium and long term?

If so, how are they monitored?

Are records kept, and are these passed on with the pupil?

Is the topic of loss included in the curriculum?

What appropriate resources do you have in relation to loss and bereavement, such as library books or a 'bereavement box'?

The pre-training quiz

The next section comprises a questionnaire for staff to complete to assess their knowledge and confidence in the area of bereavement and loss, and their training needs. It could be completed individually in a few minutes.

This could be a confidential process helping individuals to identify their confidence levels or it could be the basis for group discussions to determine overall training needs.

It is important that all staff have a basic understanding of the effect of bereavement and loss, and know the procedures and policies that are in place for responding to them. There is no need for all staff to be counsellors, but they should be aware of simple techniques such as the power of acknowledgement and of active listening.

Initially complete the school audit on pages 34–36 with senior members of staff.

Bereavement and loss: questions for senior staff

Does the school have a policy to address bereavement and loss?
If yes, when was the policy last reviewed?

Is the policy effective? Use the checklist provided to identify gaps.

Who is responsible for the area of bereavement?

Are all the staff aware of the provisions and procedures of the policy?

Which staff have received loss-awareness training or expressed an interest in developing this area?

Is loss addressed in the curriculum?

What resources relating to loss are available to staff and pupils?

Support Assessment Sheet

Consider the following pathways to identify gaps that need to be addressed:

What are the possible ways that the school could hear about the death of a parent or other significant loss?

Have these possibilities been considered and addressed in a procedure?

What actions are taken when you hear that a pupil's parent has died?

Who is responsible for contacting and liaising with the family?

What happens if a bereaved pupil is in school when news of the death arrives?

Who decides whether the school can respond to the death with its own resources? For example, is it a bereavement or critical incident?

Where is support sought if needed?

Who decides what the staff and pupils are to be told, and who liaises with the family on this issue?

How are staff and other pupils to be told of a death?

How are unaware staff alerted (e.g. part-time staff and new staff, supply teachers and those absent – ill or on courses)?

What actions are taken in the short, medium and long term after a death?

Will the family be visited and by whom?

Who will decide on actions in respect to the funeral?

Will the school be represented at the funeral? Will flowers be sent?

How are those pupils who could be emotionally affected after a death identified?

What provision is made to support these pupils?

Information about a death: questions for senior staff

Who needs to know?

Is the information accurate?

What are the communication channels?

How do you ensure that all who need to know are aware?

Why do all not need to know?

Does the family agree and are they aware who has been told and what?

The pre-training quiz

Name: _____   **Role:** _____

1. On a scale of 1 to 10, rate your knowledge of children and a significant bereavement, the possible effects and needs – 1 is low and 10 is high.

   _____

2. Briefly, what do you know about the area?

   _____

   _____

3. On a scale of 1 to 10, rate your confidence in the area of children, loss and bereavement – 1 is low and 10 is high.

   _____

4. What is your own experience of death and bereavement? How comfortable are you with the topic of death?

   _____

   _____

5. What is your experience of the following:

   • Have you ever attended a funeral?

     _____

   • Have you ever visited a chapel of rest?

     _____

   • Have you ever seen a dead body?

     _____

- Have you ever witnessed a peaceful death?

- Have you ever witnessed a traumatic death?

- Have you ever given or received bereavement counselling?

  ----

6. Does the school have a policy to address loss?

   ----

7. If yes, are you familiar with the contents of the policy?

   ----

8. Who in school is responsible for the area of bereavement?

   ----

9. Have you received any training in the area of loss and bereavement?

   ----

10. If yes, where and when?

    ----

11. What was the length of the training?

    ----

12. Did the training specifically relate to children, young people and education?

    ----

13. What do you think you need to know in the area of bereavement?

----

14. What would you do if you were contacted by a pupil's parent and told by them that the other parent had died?

----

15. What, if anything, would stop you engaging with a bereaved pupil?

----

16. How long does the period of grieving last?

----

17. What types of losses can pupils encounter?

----

18. Should pupils go to their parent's funeral?

----

19. What agencies may be able help in this area?

----

20. How can a grieving child be helped?

----

21. Are loss and bereavement addressed in the curriculum at school? If so, where and how?

_____

_____

22. Can you name any important researchers in the field of loss?

_____

_____

Pre-training quiz answers

The replies to the questions will give an idea of the level of understanding that individuals and the training needed.

1. On a scale of 1 to 10, rate your knowledge of children and a significant bereavement, the possible effects and needs – 1 is low and 10 is high.

   The answers to this question will give an approximate idea of the individual's level of understanding about the subject and when aggregated will provide an idea of overall school level.

2. Briefly, what you know about the area?

   The answer to this question will provide an idea of the level of sophistication of knowledge of individuals and may well correlate with the answers to question 1.

3. On a scale of 1 to 10, rate your confidence in the area of children, loss and bereavement – 1 is low and 10 is high.

   The answers to this question will give an approximate idea of the individual's level of confidence in the area, and when aggregated will provide an idea of overall school level.

4. What is your own experience of death and bereavement? How comfortable are you with the topic of death?

   The answers to this question give an idea of the level of experience, and potentially their level of confidence, an individual has had in the area of death and bereavement. However, not all experiences may have been positive and staff may have unresolved issues that would impact their ability to help pupils.

5. What is your experience of the following:

   • Have you ever attended a funeral?

   • Have you ever visited a chapel of rest?

   • Have you ever seen a dead body?

   • Have you ever witnessed a peaceful death?

   • Have you ever witnessed a traumatic death?

   • Have you ever given or received bereavement counselling?

   The answers to these questions, which could be scored a point for each event attended, will give an idea of the personal experience of staff. There will be a difference in experience and perhaps understanding between those scoring 0 and those scoring 6.

This may mean that they are well experienced and empathetic towards pupils, but it may also mean that they have issues about their previous experience that could inhibit their interaction with pupils.

6. Does the school have a policy to address loss?

This is to gauge the understanding of staff, and whether they know if a policy is in place. The first step of awareness for staff is to know that there is a policy in place, and this may not be the case for all.

7. If yes, are you familiar with the contents of the policy?

The second crucial step is determining whether staff know the content of any policy. If some are unaware, either of the existence of a policy and/or of its contents, then this can easily be remedied through a briefing. If the school has a policy in place, it is important that all staff are aware of the provisions.

8. Who in school is responsible for the area of bereavement?

This relates to staff being aware of a responsible person in this area who can give advice and instructions about procedures.

9. Have you received any training in the area of loss and bereavement?

10. If yes, where and when?

11. What was the length of the training?

12. Did the training specifically relate to children, young people and education?

These questions will help to identify staff who have taken an interest in this area and acquired some level of knowledge and perhaps confidence. Those already having had some training may be able to support other staff members and take the lead.

The answers provide a guide to the quality and depth of any such training, as well as the context, such as whether it related to children.

13. What do you think you need to know in the area of bereavement?

The answers to this question will provide an appraisal of the individual's training and knowledge needs in the area.

14. What would you do if you were contacted by a pupil's parent and told by them that the other parent had died?

The answer to this question will help to gauge the level of confidence and experience in the area of loss and bereavement.

15. What, if anything, would stop you engaging with a bereaved pupil?

The answers to this question will provide an insight into any barriers for individuals, and when aggregated will help to identify whether there are any patterns.

16. How long does the period of grieving last?

The answers to this question may indicate the level of sophistication that staff have in relation to the effects of bereavement. Answers that indicate it is impossible to really answer this question and that grieving may never be 'resolved', in line with the continuing bonds model, indicate a high level of sophistication. At times a two-year period has been suggested, but this is too general and does not take the individual into account, although it may indicate some knowledge in the area.

17. What types of losses can pupils encounter?

Children may encounter many losses in life, parental death being at the extreme. There are other, more numerous losses, such as when parents separate or divorce, which many children encounter. All children will at times experience the transition of moving school or class; some will move house, experience the death of a family pet or the loss of friendships; others experience being in public care and having special educational needs. All these losses will impact on pupils and on their families to a greater or lesser extent.

The more losses that are noted, the more likely it is that the individual has a broad knowledge of loss and may understand that helping children deal with the little losses that they encounter will help them cope with larger losses in life, which they are likely to encounter sooner or later.

18. Should pupils go to their parent's funeral?

This question has no simple answer. Children and young people ideally should be given the choice as to whether or not they attend and be given support and information if they do. An answer such as 'no' without any qualification indicates a low level of awareness of a pupil's needs in this area.

19. What agencies may be able help in this area?

An awareness of which agencies could potentially help also indicates a greater awareness in this area.

20. How can a grieving child be helped?

There may be many practical ways that a grieving child can be helped, especially by providing them with a listening ear, acknowledging their loss, and helping them to grieve and understand.

21. **Are loss and bereavement addressed in the curriculum at school? If so, where and how?**

    If loss is addressed in the curriculum at school, it is important that all staff are aware.

22. **Can you name any important researchers in the field of loss?**

    There are many workers in this field, and citing any will indicate a degree of knowledge in the area. Bowlby, Kubler-Ross, Murray-Parkes, Worden, Stroebe and Schut, and Bronfenbrenner are names that may be mentioned. The greater the awareness by staff of some of these workers, the more likely they are to be aware of other issues surrounding the area of loss and bereavement. Staff could be given the opportunity to read about the subject through a book list.

Evaluation of the questionnaires

Evaluating the questionnaires, through discussion or interviews, should help to identify individuals who have interest, experience or skills in the area. These could be loosely called 'experts'. At the other end of the scale are the 'novices', who may know little about the area and who may have had little experience of death or loss and will need training and support.

Training can be tailored from basic loss-awareness through to those needing a refresher course, and more complex courses for individuals involved in preparing a policy, responding to pupils and being points of contact for less confident staff.

It would be interesting to note the sources of training and the context of the training.

The questionnaire and audit could also help to identify if there is uncertainty in terms of the procedures and how to respond after a death or significant loss.

In terms of an individual's previous experience with death, the greater this experience, the more likely it is that they will be empathetic to those going through the experience as they should realise the implications. There is the potential complication that anyone who has been through a difficult experience may not necessarily be able to support a pupil who has had a similar experience.

Today, many young people may not have attended a funeral, or seen a body in any context, or witnessed a peaceful death, and this could be the case with staff at school.

Answers in relation to the school policy, if one is in place, will reveal gaps in knowledge, especially in the case of recent members of staff, but this is an issue that could be addressed through induction when they join.

CHAPTER 3

The Exercises

Training plan

After training needs have been identified, a plan can be put into action to provide appropriate training. The exercises in *Responding to Loss and Bereavement in Schools* can be used for staff without any training and knowledge to introduce the subject of loss, as well as for those needing a refresher course. The exercises can be used to begin to stimulate discussion around the current school response and to challenge, motivate and extend thinking in the area.

Training needs to be appropriate; otherwise, if it undershoots, it will not be challenging enough and will only be revision. If the training overshoots, it is too complex and may leave participants confused and lacking confidence.

Training can make a significant difference to the confidence levels of schools. In Hull, a relatively mature area with high levels of training, 58 per cent of schools seek outside help after bereavement (Holland and Wilkinson 2015b) and do not generally refer to outside agencies. Outside help may be needed if the circumstances are complex, or involve trauma or media attention.

Care must be taken with staff having recently experienced bereavement or other significant loss as their emotions may still be raw. They need care and a listening ear if they are included at all in the training exercises. Their experiences may provide valuable insight if they are able to be involved.

Types of training

The following is a list of potential training that could be identified, depending on the needs of staff:

1. Basic loss-awareness, including the effects of loss on pupils and adults.

2. A more detailed understanding of the effects of loss, the needs of pupils and how this can be reflected in policies and procedures.

3. A more detailed understanding of the needs of pupils after bereavement and development of the skills of interacting and intervening to help them, such as running peer groups, activities and listening.

4. A more detailed understanding of how to help pupils after a loss, including counselling-type skills.

Training key
Exercise groups

The exercises can be divided into groups as shown below:

Types of exercise	
Type	Exercise
Death as a taboo subject	Exercise 1: What makes a subject taboo?
	Exercise 2: Why is death a difficult or taboo subject?
Children's understanding of death	Exercise 3: Where do children get their ideas about death?
	Exercise 4: What do children understand about death?
	Exercise 5: The goldfish test
	Exercise 6: Euphemisms
	Exercise 7: Technical and complex language
	Exercise 10: Engaging with children about death
	Exercise 11: Misleading children
Experiences of death	Exercise 8: Experiences of death 1
	Exercise 9: Experiences of death 2
	Exercise 12: Different losses that pupils could experience
Responding to the family	Exercise 13: Responding to the family after a death 1
	Exercise 14: Responding to the family: the caller's perspective
	Exercise 15: Responding to the family after a death 2
	Exercise 16: A letter of condolence
	Exercise 17: A telephone call of condolence
	Exercise 18: The initial meeting with the family
	Exercise 19: When you need outside support
Funerals and the chapel of rest	Exercise 20: Children attending funerals
	Exercise 21: Parents, children and funerals
	Exercise 22: Children attending the chapel of rest
Communications in school	Exercise 23: Informing the school community
	Exercise 24: Barriers to interacting with bereaved pupils
	Exercise 25: The pupil's return to school
	Exercise 26: Support for bereaved pupils

Type	Exercise
The 'ripple' effect	Exercise 27: The 'ripple effect' after a significant death or loss 1
	Exercise 28: The 'ripple effect' after a significant death or loss 2
Helping pupils	Exercise 29: Help in the medium to long term
	Exercise 30: Warning signs
Developing a policy	Exercise 31: Bereavement policy and procedure

Potential training by role

It would be useful for all staff to gain an overall understanding in the area of bereavement, although some exercises lend themselves to one or more of the four roles (Champions, Strategists, Interventionists, Interactionists). The Champions and Strategists need a broad understanding and may already be aware of some of the issues. The Interventionists and Interactionists may not need to know about the strategic response, such as meeting the family, but there needs to be a mechanism where all staff can feed into the development of the policy.

Exercises suited to different roles	
Role	Exercise
Champions	Exercise 1: What makes a subject taboo?
	Exercise 2: Why is death a difficult or taboo subject?
	Exercise 3: Where do children get their ideas about death?
	Exercise 4: What do children understand about death?
	Exercise 5: The goldfish test
	Exercise 6: Euphemisms
	Exercise 7: Technical and complex language
	Exercise 8: Experiences of death 1
	Exercise 9: Experiences of death 2
	Exercise 10: Engaging with children about death
	Exercise 11: Misleading children
	Exercise 12: Different losses that pupils could experience
	Exercise 13: Responding to the family after a death 1
	Exercise 14: Responding to the family: the caller's perspective
	Exercise 15: Responding to the family 2
	Exercise 16: A letter of condolence
	Exercise 17: A telephone call of condolence
	Exercise 18: The initial meeting with the family

	Exercise 19: When you need outside support
	Exercise 20: Children attending funerals
	Exercise 21: Parents, children and funerals
	Exercise 22: Children attending the chapel of rest
	Exercise 23: Informing the school community
	Exercise 24: Barriers to interacting with bereaved pupils
	Exercise 25: The pupil's return to school
	Exercise 26: Support for bereaved pupils
	Exercise 27: The 'ripple effect' after a significant death or loss 1
	Exercise 28: The 'ripple effect' after a significant death or loss 2
	Exercise 29: Help in the medium to long term
	Exercise 30: Warning signs
	Exercise 31: Bereavement policy and procedure
Strategists	Exercise 1: What makes a subject taboo?
	Exercise 2: Why is death a difficult or taboo subject?
	Exercise 3: Where do children get their ideas about death?
	Exercise 4: What do children understand about death?
	Exercise 5: The goldfish test
	Exercise 6: Euphemisms
	Exercise 7: Technical and complex language
	Exercise 8: Experiences of death 1
	Exercise 9: Experiences of death 2
	Exercise 10: Engaging with children about death
	Exercise 11: Misleading children
	Exercise 12: Different losses that pupils could experience
	Exercise 13: Responding to the family after a death 1
	Exercise 14: Responding to the family: the caller's perspective
	Exercise 15: Responding to the family after a death 2
	Exercise 16: A letter of condolence
	Exercise 17: A telephone call of condolence
	Exercise 18: The initial meeting with the family
	Exercise 19: When you need outside support
	Exercise 20: Children attending funerals

Role	Exercise
	Exercise 21: Parents, children and funerals
	Exercise 22: Children attending the chapel of rest
	Exercise 23: Informing the school community
	Exercise 24: Barriers to interacting with bereaved pupils
	Exercise 25: The pupil's return to school
	Exercise 26: Support for bereaved pupils
	Exercise 27: The 'ripple effect' after a significant death or loss 1
	Exercise 28: The 'ripple effect' after a significant death or loss 2
	Exercise 29: Help in the medium to long term
	Exercise 30: Warning signs
	Exercise 31: Bereavement policy and procedure
Interventionists	Exercise 1: What makes a subject taboo?
	Exercise 2: Why is death a difficult or taboo subject?
	Exercise 3: Where do children get their ideas about death?
	Exercise 4: What do children understand about death?
	Exercise 5: The goldfish test
	Exercise 6: Euphemisms
	Exercise 7: Technical and complex language
	Exercise 8: Experiences of death 1
	Exercise 9: Experiences of death 2
	Exercise 10: Engaging with children about death
	Exercise 11: Misleading children
	Exercise 12: Different losses that pupils could experience
	Exercise 20: Children attending funerals
	Exercise 21: Parents, children and funerals
	Exercise 22: Children attending the chapel of rest
	Exercise 24: Barriers to interacting with bereaved pupils
	Exercise 25: The pupil's return to school
	Exercise 26: Support for bereaved pupils
	Exercise 27: The 'ripple effect' after a significant death or loss 1
	Exercise 28: The 'ripple effect' after a significant death or loss 2
	Exercise 29: Help in the medium to long term
	Exercise 30: Warning signs

Interactionists	Exercise 1: What makes a subject taboo?
	Exercise 2: Why is death a difficult or taboo subject?
	Exercise 3: Where do children get their ideas about death?
	Exercise 4: What do children understand about death?
	Exercise 5: The goldfish test
	Exercise 6: Euphemisms
	Exercise 7: Technical and complex language
	Exercise 8: Experiences of death 1
	Exercise 9: Experiences of death 2
	Exercise 10: Engaging with children about death
	Exercise 11: Misleading children
	Exercise 12: Different losses that pupils could experience
	Exercise 20: Children attending funerals
	Exercise 21: Parents, children and funerals
	Exercise 22: Children attending the chapel of rest
	Exercise 24: Barriers to interacting with bereaved pupils
	Exercise 25: The pupil's return to school
	Exercise 26: Support for bereaved pupils
	Exercise 27: The 'ripple effect' after a significant death or loss 1
	Exercise 28: The 'ripple effect' after a significant death or loss 2

GENERAL LOSS-AWARENESS EXERCISES

The next few exercises revolve around loss-awareness generally, and children's perceptions and understanding of death.

Exercise 1

What makes a subject taboo?

This exercise helps participants consider why death seems to be a difficult and taboo subject. The idea is to get to the heart of why a subject is considered taboo. The word 'taboo' originally came into use after Captain Cook visited Tonga, where he encountered the concept *'tapu'* relating to forbidden foods; it then became generalised to subjects other than food. Taboo relates to activities that are private or abnormal and not spoken about, such as body functions or sex. The problem with a taboo area is that while the initiated understand and have information, the uninitiated may feel excluded, puzzled and confused. You will need to prepare some 'taboo cards' as shown below; and once the activity is completed, take feedback and write the results on a flipchart or whiteboard.

Prepare the following cards:

Prepare ten cards with one word on each: five that you consider taboo in your context and five that you consider are not taboo. Some examples are given, but you can change and adapt particular words. (Female genital mutilation (FGM) is the ritual removal of some or all of the external female genitalia by a traditional circumciser using a razor.)

Death	Cancer	Sex	Incest	FGM
Water	Food	Rain	Flowers	Monkeys

Exercise 1: Activity

Individually or in pairs, discuss the taboo cards provided and rank them in order, from the most to the least controversial.

_____

_____

_____

_____

_____

_____

_____

_____

_____

_____

Then consider the following questions:

- Why are some of these words considered taboo?

- Are the words generally taboo, or only in relation to children or young people?

- Would the topics be seen as taboo in other countries around the world?

- Rate how comfortable you feel discussing the words, from 1 to 10, with 1 being the most comfortable?

- Can you express how and why you rated the words?

- Can you think of any other taboo areas?

Reflections

We all have different and varied experiences, and we live in a cultural context with our own 'norms'.

Topics and words may be taboo for the following reasons:

- The subject relates to something that is regarded as essentially private, such as certain bodily functions including sex or elimination.

- There may be an element of prohibition if the activity relates to something forbidden by religious belief or moral judgement. If an activity is forbidden, it is unlikely to be discussed openly.

- There are cultural or society 'norms' or conventions, and these may vary according to the context.

- Generally, the Victorians were comfortable with death, but not with sex, stereotypically covering up piano legs! Taboos may vary across time and between cultures.

- Topics that are considered 'taboo' may involve a lack of knowledge in the area for the uninitiated, who are unable to gain this knowledge without help from those who are aware, and this knowledge may be difficult to acquire.

- In some cultures there may be initiation ceremonies or ways of handing on this information.

Exercise 2

Why is death a difficult or taboo subject?

This activity helps participants to consider bereavement and why death may be a taboo subject. Engaging participants in discussions may open out the topic. Historically, we did not always have problems with death. This is especially true for children, who used to be involved in the rites and rituals around death and would have been aware and involved or observing. This may lead to better understanding as to why the area can be problematic in relation to communications with children. There is no clear answer as to why death is taboo, but a discussion may produce interesting issues and conversations. Some people may be comfortable discussing this area and may not consider that death is taboo at all. Take feedback, and once the exercise has been completed, write the results on a flipchart or whiteboard.

Exercise 2: Activity

Individually or in pairs, discuss the following:

- Why is death a difficult or taboo area today?
- Has death always been a difficult topic historically, and if not, why did it change?
- Is death difficult to discuss generally, or just with children?
- When have you found the area challenging?
- How could things be improved for all?

Reflections

Death can be a difficult or taboo subject for many reasons, including:

- Death became industrialised and gradually removed from the area of the family. This happened first with the undertaking profession developing in the 17th century to 'undertake' the disposal of the body. Gradually, the family lost control of the rites and rituals after death, and professionals and legislation have taken over. Nowadays, it is less likely that relations will be involved in washing the body after death or that it will remain in the home prior to burial to be visited by people paying their respects. The body may be taken to a chapel of rest, often located at the undertakers.

- Children do not have the same contact with death as in the past, when they also may have been actively involved in, or at least spectators at, death rites and rituals, so they would be aware of what was happening. Today, children may not be encouraged or welcomed at the funeral or the chapel of rest or to have contact with the body.

- Children may not learn the etiquette of death, other than that it is taboo and not to be mentioned! This contrasts with previous generations and it is therefore not surprising that myths and half-truths will develop, much as in the area of sex.

- The Victorians did not seem to have the same difficulty with death as we do, but for them sex seems to have been problematic. Some think that the impact of the World Wars of the last century and the sheer numbers of deaths have contributed to our difficulty.

- Another complication today is that it may not be easy to recognise a bereaved person. In the past there were social markers indicating that an individual had recently been bereaved – for example, people dressed in black, especially females in the close family. Today there are few social markers that somebody is bereaved; perhaps black ties are worn, but not necessarily anywhere other than at the funeral. Other markers, such as drawing the curtains and stopping the clocks, are generally not observed, or if so, only briefly.

- This may be a difficult subject, and adults having had negative experiences with death and loss may struggle with the area and be unable to facilitate or help with others' grief, including children.

Exercise 3

Where do children get their ideas about death?

This activity asks participants to recall when they first gained the idea of death, and second where children currently get these ideas. Ideally, as in the past, children learn about death from the family, but they may get ideas from the media, either in fiction or in fact, and come to regard death as being violent and scary: people are killed rather than just die.

Young children will understand about separation from their carers but have no notion of the permanency of death or the changes in body state; they may assume that the person can return to visit them and wonder how they perform bodily functions. Children may gain information from their peers in the playground or hear snatches of adult conversations, both of which may be quite distorted, with the propensity to confuse them. Take feedback, and once the exercise has been completed, write the results on a flipchart or whiteboard.

Exercise 3: Activity

Individually or in pairs, discuss the following:

- Where did you initially gain your idea and understanding of death?
- Can you remember your age at the time and what was puzzling?
- Where do children today gain their ideas and understanding about death?
- Do you think that the information children glean about death is accurate?
- Where could children potentially better gain their understanding about death?

Reflections

- Ideally, children will gain their idea and understanding about death and loss through their family. If the family has a sensitive approach, children can be helped to gain an age-appropriate level of understanding.

- In the absence of accurate information about death from the family, children may gain inaccurate information from sources such as their peers or snatches of overheard adult conversations. The things they hear, as well as how they are construed, may be confused and children may gain an incorrect perception of the facts.

- Children will gain an idea of death through the media – the front pages of newspapers and things that they see and hear on television, radio or the internet. If this happens without adult supervision and guidance, and if the children do not seek clarification, then they may form the wrong impression that death is always violent and scary, and that people are killed rather than die peacefully.

Exercise 4

What do children understand about death?

This exercise helps the participants to consider children's understanding of death, especially at different ages and how it develops into an adult level of understanding. This is important in terms of being able to respond to children's needs at the appropriate level of their understanding. Young children will understand the idea of separation but not the implications of death. Gradually, with experience and by answering questions, children will gain an adult understanding. Take feedback, and once the exercise has been completed, write the results on a flipchart or whiteboard.

Prepare the following card:

> A parent in school has recently died and the children are aged one, four, eight and twelve.
>
> Consider what each child might know about loss and bereavement. Anticipate the questions that they may ask and think about how you would explain.

Exercise 4: Activity

Individually or in pairs, discuss the following:

If children ask the questions below, what would you say?

How did Mum die?

Where is Mum?

What does dead mean?

Did I make Mum die?

When will she come back?

Will Mum come back for Christmas?

Who is looking after Mum?

Finally, is there a general consensus or disagreement in this exercise?

Reflections

- The age, maturity and experience of children are all factors relating to children's understanding about death.

- For babies who have not developed an understanding of separation, each time that a carer leaves they may or may not anticipate their return. Infants will understand the idea of separation, but will expect that parents or carers who have gone away will return eventually.

- A one-year-old is very unlikely to ask any questions.

- A 12-year-old may have an adult understanding of death and may ask questions about what happened rather than the type of questions asked by younger ones.

- Young children may have bizarre views about death and they may even see it as something that catches you if you are unlucky. Young children may be very egocentric and might think that they could have caused death, for example by saying 'I wish you were dead'.

- Younger children may not understand the changes that take place in the body state after death, and wonder how the dead person feeds or goes to the toilet.

- By the age of about seven or eight years the typical child will be gaining a near-adult understanding of death. Children who have learning or development difficulties may take longer to gain an adult understanding, and for some this may never happen.

- Children with language difficulties may take euphemisms literally and be quite confused by terms such as 'gone to sleep'. Adults may well underestimate children's understanding of death or use unhelpful and complex language or jargon and euphemisms.

- Children generally seem to be helped by being involved appropriately after the death of a close relative, thereby gaining experience in the area. Explanations given to children need to be provided in an age- and experience-related way.

- Key tips for communicating with children:

  ○ Check what the family has told the children.

  ○ Check what the family has *not* told the children.

  ○ Do not refute what a parent has said to their child; if you disagree, speak to the parent later and explain your concerns.

  ○ Find the children's level of understanding as a starting point for helping them.

  ○ Listen rather than talk.

  ○ Do not relate your own experiences unless specifically asked.

  ○ Do not put a positive spin on the death.

  ○ Say if you do not know the answer, but also say that you will try to find out.

  ○ Keep any promises that you make to pupils, or their families.

  ○ Stick to age-appropriate language when speaking to the pupil.

  ○ Do not use euphemisms, jargon or confusing language.

  ○ Use games or activities, including writing and drawing, for pupils to explain their feelings.

Exercise 5

The goldfish test

The goldfish test is an exercise to help participants understand how everyday experiences can be used to help children gain an understanding of loss in life. An initial reaction may be to shield children from any loss, but in so doing they are losing an experience of coping with an emotional response in a relatively safe way. If the children find a dead animal or a dead pet, then changing the subject and not answering their questions will not help them gain understanding. If they are sensitively helped through small losses, recognising and exploring the feelings and emotions that arise, this will help them to gain a better and more realistic understanding of death and loss. Take feedback, and once the exercise has been completed, write the results on a flipchart or whiteboard.

Exercise 5: Activity

One day you go to a fair with your children and win a goldfish in a 'hook the duck' competition. The next day when you go downstairs the goldfish is dead. The children are still upstairs in bed and there are no signs of them waking up.

What would you do?
Some options are shown below. What are the consequences of each option, or any other, to the children's understanding of death?

1. Dash down to the pet shop to buy a suitable replacement.
2. Flush the goldfish down the toilet and deny all knowledge.
3. Let the children come downstairs and find the goldfish dead.
4. Dispose of the goldfish and then say that the cat must have eaten it, or that it has been taken by aliens.
5. Any other ideas?

Discuss the following in pairs or in groups:

- Have you had a similar experience as a child, or as an adult with a child?
- Consider the options and the advantages and disadvantages of each one.
- Which option would you choose?
- What could be the long-term implications of shielding children from all forms of loss?

Reflections

- Choosing an option other than No. 3 removes the opportunity of giving children the experience of a relatively small loss.

- Children may well be upset, but they are learning about the emotions of loss and this may be helpful when they encounter greater losses later in life.

- Children have the potential to learn about death and loss through everyday experiences such as finding a dead hedgehog on the road.

- If their questions are ignored or not answered, then an opportunity has been lost.

- The language used with children needs to be related to their state of development and understanding, and not too complex.

- If possible, the correct terminology should be used – for example, that the goldfish is dead or has died, rather than using a euphemism. Young children may not fully understand the term 'dead', but they have the basis for developing the concept as they mature.

Exercise 6

Euphemisms

This exercise alerts participants to the risks that euphemisms play in potentially confusing children. Euphemisms are found in taboo areas where we may feel uncomfortable, such as bodily functions or sex; this is also the case with death.

Adults are well aware of the meaning behind euphemisms such as 'pushing up daisies', but children may take these literally and not connect them with a death. For children with language difficulties and those who take language literally, euphemisms can be very confusing. For example, when they hear that King Charles was beheaded, they may wonder how a king could have a bee's head! Take feedback, and once the exercise has been completed, write the results on a flipchart or whiteboard.

Exercise 6: Activity

Individually, in pairs or through a brainstorm, discuss:

- How many euphemisms can you think of that relate to death?
- Were you confused by any particular euphemisms when you were a child?
- What could be the origin of particular euphemisms?
- How can particular euphemisms be confusing for children?
- Why are there euphemisms at all?
- Does age play a part in confusing children?

Reflections

- Euphemisms are used to 'soften' a difficult subject, and while they may be understood by adults, they may confuse children.

- Younger children and those with communication issues, such as autism spectrum disorders, may be especially confused. These pupils may take euphemisms literally and potentially be quite frightened by phrases such as 'going to sleep' or 'taken by Jesus'.

- *'Gone to heaven'*: Care needs to be taken not to confuse religious beliefs with euphemisms – in this example, 'gone to heaven' is a belief for many and is therefore literal. Care needs to be taken to ensure that children are not confused and think, for example, that heaven is a place from which the deceased can return to visit.

- *'Gone to live with the angels'*: Again, this is a religious belief, but care needs to be taken to ensure that children do not think that the deceased has chosen to leave the family and live elsewhere, which may seem like a rejection.

- *'Gone to sleep'*: When combined with the usage in relation to animals being euthanised, this has the potential to make children frightened to go to sleep.

- *'Lost'*: If the dead person is described as being 'lost', this gives the impression that the deceased will return when they are found, or that death and being lost are equivalent. This may then cause children alarm if somebody is literally lost.

- *'A star in the sky'*: This makes things difficult if at the same time relatives are visiting the grave to lay flowers. It may sound like quite an isolated and lonely state.

- *'Taken by Jesus'*: Although this may be a religious belief, it also gives the impression that someone has been abducted. This may make children wary – for example, they may be reluctant to go to church in case they experience the same fate.

- *'Six feet under'*: This is a literal euphemism, which may be quite meaningless but confusing to children or possibly scary. Children may not necessarily relate this to a coffin being in a grave.

- *'Pushing up daisies'*: This is another euphemism related to graves, or being in the earth, which may be quite meaningless but confusing to children, who could think that it relates to gardening.

- *'Snuffed it'*: This was a far more meaningful metaphor before the advent of gas and electric lighting. Today, with candles not so much in common usage, other than in churches, it may have very little meaning for children and confuse them.

- *'Kicked the bucket'*: The origin of the euphemism seems to relate either to an execution, where a bucket is kicked from under the person's feet to cause death by hanging, or to the killing of pigs, where a bucket was placed below the animal to collect blood, and the bucket kicked by the death throw of the pig. This also may have little meaning for children today.

- *'Carked it'*: This, apparently, is an ANZAC (Australian and New Zealand Army Corps) black humour slang term from the wars of the last century, referring to being a carcass and therefore dead!

- *'At rest'*: This euphemism also gives the idea that the deceased is resting somewhere, and children may wonder why they do not stop their rest and return.

- *'Passed on'* or *'Passed over'*: This has become a common euphemism and relates to the religious idea of moving on to the 'next life'. The danger is that it may be both meaningless and confusing to children.

Communication with children needs to be at their level of understanding and development – for example, young children may relate to a simple explanation that the person has died, but be confused by euphemisms. As they mature and become indoctrinated into the adult world, they will develop the skills to 'read between the lines', although it is hoped that they themselves will use less confusing language!

Exercise 7

Technical and complex language

This exercise helps to make participants aware of the language that they choose to use when communicating with the bereaved, especially with children who have language or development difficulties impeding their understanding. The use of technical, complex language and jargon has the potential to confuse children. Any communication with bereaved children needs to be clear, and it is necessary to make sure that they fully understand the words that you are using about the death. Lack of understanding surrounding a death can lead to children feeling isolated, excluded and confused. Take feedback, and once the exercise has been completed, write the results on a flipchart or whiteboard.

Exercise 7: Activity

In pairs or groups, consider the terms below and how they have the potential to be confusing for children. These are words that children may hear being used by doctors, nurses and hospital staff, or by family members discussing the circumstances around a death.

Through a brainstorm, discuss:

- heart attack
- stroke
- terminal illness
- cardiac arrest
- AIDS
- cancer
- ventilator
- CAT scan.

Reflections

- *Heart attack:* Describing a death in this way may confuse children as they may wonder how and why a heart can be attacked and by whom.

- *Stroke:* A stroke is something generally gentle – you may stroke a kitten. To hear that somebody has died from a stroke may confuse and frighten children.

- *Terminal illness:* This could be connected with going on holiday if children have experience of or have heard about airport terminals. To have an illness relating to an actual airport location may be frightening.

- *Cardiac arrest:* The potential for misunderstanding here is that children may think that the dead person is really at a police station 'helping the police'.

- *AIDS:* Children encounter 'aids' at school, in the context of teaching assistants and equipment to help pupils with difficulties. That you can die of AIDS may be quite counterintuitive to children.

- *Cancer:* 'Cancer' is a word that seems as taboo as the word 'death'. If the word is used, it is highly likely that children will not understand it at all, but they may be frightened by the way adults use it.

- *Serial killer:* This is understood by adults, but children may wonder how something that they may think you eat for breakfast can kill you.

- *The body is in the coffin:* Simple statements have the propensity to confuse children as they may wonder: If the body is in the coffin, where are the head and limbs?

- *Ventilator:* This may confuse children as the term generally relates to opening a window or letting air into a room.

- *CAT scan:* Children may wonder why cats are involved at hospital, and may even connect them with strokes.

Communication with children needs to be at their level of understanding and development. Young children may understand that a body part is worn out, but be totally confused by a complex medical explanation. As children mature, they will develop the capacity to understand more complex medical terms.

Exercise 8

Experiences of death 1

Adults have a wealth of historical experience that they could potentially use to help bereaved children. We all have different experiences and encounters with death, and participants are encouraged to discuss their negative and positives experiences, and what helped compared with what hindered them. Some individuals may have had difficult experiences that they may not wish to share, but if they can, this may help others to gain an insight into the effects of loss on adults and the potential effect on children. The participants should be cautioned only to share things that they feel comfortable with, and care needs to be taken if anyone becomes upset or distressed. Take feedback, and once the exercise has been completed, write the results on a flipchart or whiteboard.

Exercise 8: Activity

In pairs, share any previous experiences in the area of loss and death that you are comfortable to discuss with others.

This could relate to:

- attending a funeral
- visiting a chapel of rest
- visiting relations after a death

Discuss your thoughts in a group:

- What things helped and what things hindered your experiences?
- How could these experiences be used to help pupils?

Reflections

We each have our own individual experiences of loss and death. No two people will have identical experiences, and how we perceive each loss depends on things like our personality, the state of our life at the time of the loss and how we have dealt with previous encounters with loss. Because of this individuality, avoid saying to a bereaved adult or child that you know 'exactly how they feel', as clearly you cannot know this.

On the other hand, there may be many things that we have in common with others after a loss – for example, an element of shock and surprise initially, followed by a period of orientation and adjustment to the loss. It may also help to talk things through with others and have empathetic listeners.

Having experienced a significant loss can alert you to the complex nature of loss and give at least a superficial idea of what another person has been through, such as shock and denial.

The best approach is to ask the bereaved person how they are feeling and, if necessary and appropriate, reassure them that their feelings are normal.

Adults may have had a rich experience of life; the ability to see things in perspective and your experience and insights may help you respond to the bereavement.

Care needs to be taken not to relate your own loss experiences to the bereaved person unless you are specifically asked, and then only if you are comfortable in doing so.

Exercise 9

Experiences of death 2

This exercise is an alternative to the previous one and uses adult experiences to gain empathy and insights into how the bereaved may be helped. The exercise relates to the level of encounters that adults have had in the area of death. We all have different experiences of and encounters with death, and discussions about the negative and positives experiences of the participants, and what helped or hindered them, could be valuable lessons in helping pupils. The participants should be cautioned only to share things that they feel comfortable with, and care needs to be taken if any become upset or distressed. Take feedback, and once the exercise has been completed, write the results on a flipchart or whiteboard.

Prepare the following cards:

Prepare six number cards, each with a number from 1 to 6 on it, and place them, in order, at regular intervals around the room.

Attended a funeral.	Given or received bereavement counselling.	Attended a chapel of rest.
Seen a dead body.	Witnessed a peaceful death.	Witnessed a traumatic death.

Exercise 9: Activity

There are six cards (numbered 1 to 6) in the room, which correspond with different experiences related to death. Look at the list of points below, see which experiences apply to you, then move to the *highest* corresponding number card in the room.

1. If you have ever attended a funeral.

2. If you have ever given or received bereavement counselling.

3. If you have ever attended a chapel of rest.

4. If you have ever seen a dead body.

5. If you have ever witnessed a peaceful death.

6. If you have ever witnessed a traumatic death.

Then discuss in pairs:

- How did you feel about your numbered experience?

- Was it more or less difficult than you had expected?

- What things helped you with the experiences?

- What things hindered you with the experiences?

Share your thoughts with the group:

- How similar or different were the experiences of all?

Reflections

Each individual has their own experience of loss and death, as well as their own level of involvement, which could vary considerably from being with an individual when they died to not having attended a funeral.

No two people will have identical experiences and how we perceive each loss depends on such as our personality, the state of our life at the time of the loss and how we have dealt with previous encounters with loss.

Having had particular experiences of involvement with death will give an insight into ways that the bereaved may be helped, and discussion about what helped or hindered could be useful to other participants and to helping pupils.

Care needs to be taken not to relate your own experiences to pupils unless asked and then only if you are comfortable doing so.

There may be many things that we have in common with others after a loss, for example an element of shock and surprise initially, and that it can take time taken to orientate and adjust to the loss. It may also help to talk things through with others and have empathetic listeners.

Having experience a significant loss can alert you to the complex nature of loss and give at least a superficial idea of what they have been through, such as shock and denial.

Avoid saying to a bereaved adult or child that you know 'exactly how you feel', as clearly you cannot know how they feel.

The best approach is to ask the bereaved person how they are feeling and if necessary and appropriate reassure them that their feelings are normal.

Adults may have had a rich experience of life and the ability to see things in perspective and your experience and insights may help you respond to the bereavement.

Care needs to be taken not to relate your own loss experiences to the bereaved person unless you are specifically asked and then only it you are comfortable in so doing.

Exercise 10

Engaging with children about death

Children in the 'Iceberg' study found that some adults were not approachable at school, and sometimes they had nobody to listen to them either at home or school. Some bereaved pupils felt very isolated. This exercise helps the participants to identify possible reasons why this could be the case, which may be helpful in reducing the barriers to engaging with the bereaved. Take feedback and write the results on a flipchart or whiteboard.

> ## Exercise 10: Activity
>
> Discuss in pairs or small groups:
> - Is it important in principle for someone to engage with the bereaved pupil?
> - What are the reasons for your answer?
> - What things could prevent you from engaging with a bereaved pupil?
> - How could these barriers to engagement be reduced?
> - If you have no barriers yourself, what barriers could others have that prevent them from engaging with the bereaved?

Reflections

- Death may be a taboo subject and be a barrier that can inhibit interactions and conversations generally, and especially with a pupil. Being open and discussing the area generally could actually help pupils to demystify the subject, although care must be taken in specifics to ensure that the family's views are not contradicted. If a difficult situation seems to be developing then it is best to say that you will find out and consult with the family.

- There may be a fear that discussing the topic will be upsetting for children and young people. Care needs to be taken about the context, and if pupils become upset or distressed it is necessary to ensure their wellbeing.

- Adults may underestimate children's understanding of loss and death and decide not to say anything. Children will understand explanations at their level of understanding and experience. There is no need for complex explanations in medical terms, which may only confuse. An explanation that a part of the body is 'worn out' or 'tired' may be sufficient for a young child, and can be built on later as their understanding develops.

- There is the danger of an 'elephant in the room' situation, in that nobody will talk to anybody through fear of upsetting others. This could mean that children and adults both want to talk, but fail to through concerns that they may cause upset. Adults are in the best position to break this circle by making the first approach to children.

- There is an interesting fiction book for children titled *Not Now Bernard*, which shows adults missing or ignoring cues that children want to say something important to them.

- There can be a view that it is better if children don't know, and therefore they should not be included in discussions about death. The danger with this approach is that children may well feel excluded, they may gain information through other routes, which may be inaccurate, or they may make up their own myths and fantasies around the death, which could be far worse than the actuality. It would be best to include children from the beginning, in terms that they can understand.

- A worry for adults in relation to death is that they may be unsure of what to say, and this could be compounded when engaging with children. The danger is that being unsure of what to say may lead individuals not to respond at all, which may leave the bereaved thinking that the individual either doesn't know or doesn't care.

Exercise 11

Misleading children

In this exercise the participants are helped to gain insight into the danger of minimising a serious situation and later having to explain a death. One participant plays the role of a parent trying to reassure the child about the other parent, who has been involved in a road collision. It also challenges the language used in explaining things to children. Participants are allocated to be either a parent or child; if there is an odd number, there could be two children in one of the groups. Participants are asked to recall incidents when they were misled in similar situations. Allow 5–10 minutes for this activity. Take feedback, and once the exercise has been completed, write the results on a flipchart or whiteboard.

Prepare the following cards:

Parent 1

You are a parent and your partner has been involved in a serious road traffic collision. They are badly injured in intensive care, and the doctors have warned you that they may not survive. Your child wants to know what is happening, but you don't want to alarm them and so minimise the seriousness. You may need to think of a scenario to embellish the bare facts and be prepared to ad-lib!

Your task is to minimise the incident and make light of it.

Child 1

You are a child and know that one of your parents has been involved in a road traffic collision, but you know nothing of the details. Try to elicit this information from your parent. Your parent seems reluctant to share any information and you become more and more concerned!

Parent 2

A few hours later, your partner dies and you have to explain the death to your child, who thinks that there is little wrong. What would you say to them in light of the first part of the exercise?

Child 2

You still want to know more about the details of your parent's condition and are not at all happy. Continue to press your parent.

Exercise 11: Activity

Read the card that you are allocated: it will be either a Parent 1 card or a Child 1 card. Do not share the information on it with anybody who has a different role. After 5–10 minutes repeat this activity in the same role but with the Parent 2 card and the Child 2 card.

Then discuss:

- How did you feel in your role?
- What are the disadvantages and advantages of parents acting as in the first card?
- How did it feel either to explain the death after minimising the situation, or as a child to be misled and then suddenly find out the truth?
- What were there differences between the role of the parent and the child?
- What would have made you feel better, or worse?
- Were you ever misled in a similar way as a child?
- If so, what would have helped?

Reflections

- Ideally, children should be told the truth in terms that they can understand. It is important to gain an idea of their level of understanding – this could be by interacting with them and then pitching your level of interaction appropriately.

- If children are not told the truth in language and concepts that they can understand, they may have to suddenly come to terms with a major adjustment in their mind-sets.

- Children will find out the truth sooner or later, and if they feel misled by adults, they may find it more difficult to trust them in the future.

- Use appropriate language with children, making it clear and avoiding euphemisms and complex medical terms or jargon.

- Be prepared to answer questions if children want to know more information. If you do not know, then say so, but add that you will try to find out.

- Always be careful to check what the family has told children and to liaise with them if appropriate.

Exercise 12

Different losses that pupils could experience

This exercise is designed to help to broaden the participants' ideas of loss and the potential effect on pupils, and it can be used as part of a loss-awareness training session. The participants are partly engaged with the losses that they encountered as children, and they should gain a greater idea of the potential areas of loss for pupils and staff, extending well beyond loss through death. Take feedback, and once the exercise has been completed, write the results on a flipchart or whiteboard.

Exercise 12: Activity

Think of your own childhood experiences of loss – those that you feel comfortable sharing (it could be a move of house or a death in the family, including pets). Choose a specific loss and discuss in pairs:

- How old were you at the time?
- Can you recall your feelings at the time?
- At the time what helped and what hindered?
- Why do you think that this particular loss came to mind? Why was it significant?

In larger groups, discuss:

- What types of losses have the other participants experienced?
- Were the losses similar or different in each pair?
- What types of losses could pupils at school experience?
- Do you think that pupils' experiences of loss will be similar to your own, or different?
- Using your own experiences, what do you think could help or hinder pupils at school when they experience losses?

Reflections

- Loss is a normal part of life; we live in constant change or flux, as we move through time and experience changes.

- Any change can potentially be problematic, but it is when the change becomes overwhelming that it causes the greater difficulties.

- Individuals have different thresholds and levels of resilience, maturity and experiences, and these potentially impact on a current loss, either in a positive or negative way.

- A difficult past experience may lead to greater empathy and understanding of others currently going through loss. However, you may find that your own memories and old issues are revived, making it more difficult to help the bereaved.

- Some pupils at school may already have experienced quite significant losses. *Responding to Loss and Bereavement in Schools* provides a framework for addressing any of these losses. Loss is rarely a one-dimensional event, and further losses may flow from the original loss and impact on the life of the pupil.

- Many pupils will have experienced their parents separating and divorcing, perhaps in very difficult circumstances. Parental separation is a far more common loss experience for children than parental bereavement.

- Pupils may already have experienced the death of a close relative, such as a grandparent, although the school may be unaware and may not have been informed.

- Some pupils will have experienced difficulties such as being in public care; they may be an incomer, perhaps from an area of conflict abroad; or they may have attachment issues; other pupils may have a parent in prison and not have much contact with them, as well as feeling stigmatised.

- Many pupils, and also adults, experience the death of a pet. This may be a highly significant event for them, which is not always fully recognised by others.

- Family life also involves change – for example, a move of house can mean the loss of neighbours and friendships, and for children a move of school. The birth of a baby involves change, as will a new partner or marriage. Having a baby will mean that there is less time for the current children, and remarriage after a parental separation may be very difficuly for children, as not only may they lose contact with the birth parent, but also their remaining parent will be devoting time to their new partner. Friendships and other relationships may wax and wane. All these events involve changes and losses as well as gains that may impact on the family and children.

- The effect of illness or disability may be unrecognised as a loss. Disability by definition means changes in expectations and an emotional reaction to the loss.

THE INITIAL RESPONSES TO A DEATH

The next exercises move into the area of a death or significant loss having taken place and potential issues around the school response to pupil bereavement.

Exercise 13

Responding to the family after a death 1

This exercise encourages participants to consider how to respond when a family member phones or contacts the school to report the death of a pupil's parent. A telephone call or contact after a death may come 'out of the blue' and it may be difficult initially for you to process and absorb the information. The caller may also be in a state of shock and distressed, even if the death is expected after a long illness, and it may be one of the first calls that they make. Offering condolences, gaining the relevant information and offering help, including further contact, are all things that could be useful, although the possibilities and options need consideration before a call is received and at a time of calm when policies and procedures are prepared and discussed. The exercise can be used in terms of training as well as to test the robustness of established systems, and to help to look for 'bugs' or gaps in the system. Take feedback, and once the exercise has been completed, write the results on a flipchart or whiteboard.

Prepare the following card:

> A parent calls to say that the previous evening the other parent was involved in a road traffic accident and later died in hospital. The family now comprises one parent and two children, one of whom attends your school. The parent is in a state of shock and is currently contacting relations, but is unclear about what to do next.

Exercise 13: Activity

Read the card, reflect individually and discuss in pairs or in a small group:

- Who would be likely to receive the news at school?

- How prepared would they be?

- How could they be further prepared?

- How would you currently respond to such a contact?

- What information would you seek?

- What information do you need?

- Is there anything that you could do to improve the current response?

- Are there any training issues?

Reflections

- The response to the news of the death of a pupil's parent is important as it potentially sets the tone for the rest of the relationship around the death.

- Care needs to be taken to be sensitive and empathetic as well as recording relevant details.

- If there is nobody appropriate currently available at school to respond, contact details need to be taken and passed on to ensure speedy responses.

- Obtaining at least brief details of the circumstances will help you to decide whether the death is one that can be dealt with without external support. If trauma is involved, such as pupils witnessing a death, specialist outside help may be needed quickly, as is also the case if there is media interest.

- The caller may be quite shocked by the news of the death, even if it had been anticipated. Sympathies should be extended and the caller should be asked if the family needs immediate help. If the news is recent, then the details may be initially scarce and sketchy.

- The person receiving the call or visit may themselves be shocked by the news, and there is the danger of not eliciting sufficient details from the caller.

- Bereaved pupils at school will ideally need to be collected by the family, who are best placed to break the initial news to their children.

- An acknowledgment stating that you are sorry to hear the news is important.

- If there is a system or procedure in place at school whereby a particular member of staff liaises with the family, then this needs to be activated.

- Keeping a link with the family will help them and the pupils, and the school can later offer guidance or help if this is requested.

Exercise 14

Responding to the family: the caller's perspective

In this exercise the participants are asked to look at the perceptions and feelings of the person who is making contact with the school. The caller may be quite distressed after the death. Those receiving a call need to have a tactful and sensitive response and have empathy with the caller, who may be going through a very difficult and emotional time. Potential receivers of telephone calls or visiting callers need challenging to consider what they would expect and need if they were the caller, and this may help in developing the school response. Take feedback, and once the exercise has been completed, write the results on a flipchart or whiteboard.

Prepare the following card:

> A parent calls to say that the previous evening the other parent was involved in a road traffic accident and later died in hospital. The family now comprises one parent and two children, one of whom attends your school. The parent is in a state of shock and is currently contacting relations but is unclear as what to do next. They are clearly emotionally distressed and at times find it difficult to talk.

Exercise 14: Activity

Read the card, reflect individually and discuss in pairs or in a small group:

- Have you had a similar experience, either being the caller or the called?

- How did it feel and what helped and hindered?

- How would the caller be feeling when making the call or the visit?

- How would the caller feel if they were unable to speak to an appropriate person?

- What could you do to help them?

- How would they feel if they were able to speak to somebody in the management team?

- What would the caller expect to happen next?

- What questions might the caller ask?

- What questions might you ask?

Discuss with the group and compare your findings:

- Were these similar or different?

- If so, how?

Reflections

- The response to the news of the death of a pupil's parent is important as it sets the tone for the rest of the relationship around the death.

- Care needs to be taken to be sensitive and empathetic as well as recording relevant details.

- If there is nobody appropriate currently available at school to respond, contact details need to be taken and passed on to ensure speedy responses.

- Obtaining at least brief details of the circumstances will help you to decide whether the death is one that can be dealt with without external support. If trauma is involved, such as pupils witnessing a peer's death, specialist outside help may be needed quickly, as is also the case if there is significant media interest.

- The caller may be quite shocked, even if the death had been anticipated. Sympathies should be extended and the caller asked whether the family needs immediate help. If the news is recent, then details may be scarce and sketchy, and will emerge later.

- Bereaved pupils at school will need to be collected by family members, who are best placed to break the initial news to their children.

- An acknowledgment stating that you are sorry to hear the news is important.

- If there is a system or procedure in place at school whereby a particular member of staff liaises with the family, then this needs to be activated.

- Keeping a link with the family will help them and the pupil, and the school can later offer guidance or help if this is requested.

Exercise 15

Responding to the family after a death 2

This exercise is designed to help the participants gain insight into what might help a family after a death, using their own experiences of bereavement to discuss what responses could be made to the family after the news has been received in school. How could contact be made and who will be involved? Take feedback, and once the exercise has been completed, write the results on a flipchart or whiteboard.

Exercise 15: Activity

Discuss in pairs or in a small group:

- Have you had a close bereavement?
- If so, do you recall what initially was helpful to you?
- If not, can you think of what might be helpful for the family?
- How could the family be contacted?
- What are the best ways of making and keeping in contact?
- What would you say during any contact?
- What information do you need?
- What could the family ask?
- What currently happens and is it addressed in a policy document?

Discuss your thoughts in groups:

- Was there a general agreement as to what was likely to be helpful?
- What were the differences and why did they arise?

Reflections

- There are a range of responses that a school can make after they have been made aware of the death of a family member.

- Personal contact is preferable, by telephoning and arranging an initial visit to the family home or meeting them at a convenient location of their choice. A telephone conversation is the next best contact if it is not possible to arrange a meeting.

- Other forms of contact include writing a letter or sending a card of condolence, which could be done in addition to personal contact.

- Remember that this is a home in mourning and it is important to acknowledge the bereavement, offer condolences, and ask if you can help in any way.

- It could be prudent for two staff to make the initial visit and to make follow-up visits either individually or in pairs, whichever is considered preferable.

- Be prepared for the family to seek advice, especially relating to the children. If you are unsure about what to say, or do not know, say that you will try to find out and then contact the family quickly with an answer or suggestion as to another avenue of enquiry.

- It is helpful to ask the family about details of the death and what the children have been told. Children should be given information that is honest and appropriate to their age, maturity and level of understanding. It is best not to mislead children or tell them things that they may later find out are wrong. Not telling the truth will lead children not to trust adults and may provoke an angry response if they feel that they have been deliberately misled.

- It would be helpful if there is a discussion and agreement with the family as to what to tell the rest of the school. This may be just to inform the school community about the death. It would be unrealistic to assume that the news is not known in the community – rumours will usually abound.

- If there is clarity, then bereaved pupils will return to school not worrying about who knows about the death.

- It is helpful to know the date of the funeral in order that the school can consider making a response by attending or sending a wreath or flowers. The family may request that only the family sends flowers and ask for donations to an appropriate charity, in which case a collection could be made at school.

- It would be useful to gain an idea as to how long, if at all, the pupil will be off school. It may be difficult to know initially, but there needs to be a carefully planned transition for the pupil back to school. This could be either a phased or a total return.

Exercise 16

A letter of condolence

In this exercise the participants are asked to draft a letter of condolence. Ask them to write something individually and then to share its content with a partner or group. This exercise is difficult in that a letter of condolence needs to be personal and relate to the context, and so it may seem contrived. Drafting a letter may help to clarify thoughts, and a draft could be included in any policy document to provide a starting point for a response. Take feedback, and once the exercise has been completed, write the results on a flipchart or whiteboard.

Exercise 16: Activity

Individually, draft a letter of condolence to a family after a death.

- Discuss your letter in pairs or a small group.
- Were the letters similar or different?
- If they were different, in which ways?
- What are the key components of a letter?
- Is it helpful to have a letter drafted and as part of a policy?
- If yes, how?
- If no, why not?

Reflections

- Any letter needs to be thought through individually and will depend on the circumstances and the family.

- The letter needs to offer condolences as well as help if needed.

- It is useful to have thought this through before it is needed, and a draft letter gives you a basis to work from.

- Avoid giving any hint of a positive aspect to the death, such as that the deceased is no longer in pain.

- Avoid suggesting that the bereaved could have done something different, such as calling an ambulance earlier.

- The shorter, simpler and to the point the better, especially as further details of the death may come to light later.

The following is an example, although the actual letter needs to be written at the time of the death and bear in mind what you then want to say.

Dear Mr Brown,

We were all very sorry to hear about the death of your wife, and the school community extends our sympathy and condolences at this difficult time.

I will telephone you shortly to see if we can help, and in the meantime do not hesitate to contact me if we can help in any way.

Yours sincerely,

Head Teacher

The formality and tone will depend on the circumstances and your relationship with the family.

Exercise 17

A telephone call of condolence

It may be necessary or appropriate to make the initial contact with the family by telephone. This exercise enables the participants to have thought through what to say to the family before a call is needed. If notes of potential points are made, this may help participants to be better prepared to make such a call. A call, like a letter, needs to be a human and humane link and should not be read as a script, although it is useful to have a list of points to be raised. Take feedback, and once the exercise has been completed, write the results on a flipchart or whiteboard.

Prepare the following card:

> Office staff received a telephone call from a distressed parent saying that their partner has been killed in a road traffic accident. In line with the policy, as nobody was available at the time, the office staff took the message, obtained a contact number, and said that the parent would be contacted as soon as possible.

Exercise 17: Activity

Individually:

- Read the card.

- Make notes of what you would say in a telephone call of condolence.

Discuss your notes in a small group:

- Are your points similar?

- Are your points in the same order?

- Is it helpful to have some notes drafted and forming part of a policy?

- If yes, why?

- If not, why not?

Reflections

- A telephone response needs to be well thought through in advance and not read out as a script. The call is individual and will depend on the circumstances and the family, although it would be helpful to have a list of points that you need to raise.

- Care needs to be taken that the time is suitable for the family, even if the time has been previously arranged. You could always offer to call back at a more convenient time.

- The telephone call needs to offer condolences as well as offering help if needed. Words such as 'I was very sorry to hear about the death' may be helpful, but, as with a letter, need to be short.

- Avoid giving any hint of a positive aspect to the death, such as that the deceased is no longer in pain.

- Avoid suggesting that the bereaved could have done something else, such as call an ambulance earlier.

- The shorter, simpler and to the point the better, as the family may be very busy making arrangements.

The following is an example of draft telephone call points:

- Ask if it is a convenient time to speak, and if not, ask when would be more convenient.

- Offer condolences, saying that you are sorry to hear about the death, in words that are appropriate at the time.

- Ask the family if you can visit them at home.

- Ask if there is any other way that you can help.

- Ensure that the family feels comfortable to contact you for help.

- Arrange a follow-up call or visit.

- Initially it may be too early to discuss the funeral and other rites, unless this is raised by the family.

Exercise 18

The initial meeting with the family

This exercise will help to prepare the participants for the initial meeting that they have with the family. The first meeting after the death is important in setting the tone for the relationship between the school and the family and in developing trust and good communications. The participants can draw on their own experiences. You will likely be anxious when calling on a bereaved family, and it can help for two people to attend at least the first meeting. From the perspective of the family, they will be feeling 'raw' after the death, perhaps distressed, and your response could have a positive effect if you are able to provide guidance and reassurance. Take feedback, and once the exercise has been completed, write the results on a flipchart or whiteboard.

Prepare the following cards:

Parent

You are a parent and your partner has unexpectedly died after a short illness (this you can construct and elaborate on). You feel overwhelmed and are unsure about how your children, aged five, six and eleven, will manage.

You would welcome support but are unsure where to find it.

You are unsure as to whether the children should attend the funeral and how long they should stay off school, if at all.

You contacted the school by telephone, and the head teacher is coming for a first home visit but you are unsure if they are coming alone.

Your task is to try to elicit the above information and anything else that could be appropriate in the circumstances.

School staff member

You are the head teacher of the local primary school and have been contacted by a parent saying that their partner has recently died after a short illness.

You have no details of the death other than it was after a short illness. There are three children, aged five, six and eleven, at your school.

Think about what you would say to the parent and what advice you could give if asked.

Spend a little time thinking about the information that you need to obtain.

Exercise 18: Activity

Read the card that you are allocated – it will be either a parent or staff member card – without sharing the information with somebody having a different role. After taking 5–10 minutes to consider both circumstances and the information to be obtained or given, discuss the following in pairs or in a small group:

- If you have been bereaved, were the words that people used helpful?
- Which words did you find not so helpful?
- Which words do you wish people had used?
- Which words do you wish people had not used?
- What words could you use when first meeting with a bereaved family?
- What information do you need from the family?
- What questions could the family ask?
- How did the exercise make you feel?

Reflections

- Any verbal response needs to be well thought through and will depend on the circumstances and the family.

- Ideally, a visit or meeting should involve two school members.

- You could acknowledge the loss, such as by saying that you are sorry to hear about the death, and offer help.

- It could be useful to have considered a strategy before it is needed, and have planned a basic approach that could be adapted to circumstances.

- The family may ask for help and it would be prudent to have already considered what help might be available, such as in the community or neighbourhood.

- The family may ask what the children should be told, whether they should attend the funeral and when they should return to school. It may be that the family has already decided, but using the information that you have previously considered, you could be in the position of being able to offer guidance.

Exercise 19

When you need outside support

This exercise will help alert participants to the circumstances when they need to seek outside support. In most cases a school will be able to provide support from its own resources. At times this may not be possible – for example, if the death attracts media attention and the school is being inundated with requests for information and interviews. There may have been a death on the school premises and there may be trauma involved, in relation to what staff or pupils have seen or heard. In these cases it would be prudent to seek advice. The local authority may be able to provide support in relation to the media, and there could be a specific member of staff tasked with a liaison role. In the case of trauma, such as where pupils have witnessed a death, the local authority may have a crisis team that could assist, as could health services. Take feedback, and once the exercise has been completed, write the results on a flipchart or whiteboard.

Prepare the following card:

A parent is killed in an accident over the half-term holiday.

A staff member commits suicide on the school premises late at night outside school hours.

A parent is killed in a terrorist incident abroad and there is a media circus outside the school, with calls from reporters for interviews.

A parent dies in a local hospice after a long illness.

Exercise 19: Activity

Read the card and discuss in pairs or in a small group in which circumstances you may need to call in outside help, or you feel that the school could manage using its own resources. What are the reasons for your answers?

Now consider the following:

- Can you think of any other circumstances when you may need to seek outside support after bereavement?

- Where would you seek outside support?

- Do you currently have any links that could potentially provide support and guidance, such as through the school's educational psychologist?

Reflections

- Critical incidents: If there has been a high level of trauma (e.g. staff and pupils either witnessing a death or having been unduly frightened), specialist support may be needed from psychologists or from the local authority or health authority.

- There can be a high level of trauma without there being an actual death, where specialist support is still needed. For example, when the school community feels threatened by violence, perhaps by somebody on the site with a knife or a gun.

- Most bereavement does not involve trauma in the sense of individuals being put in fear of their lives, although the death of someone significant will evoke emotional reactions such as shock.

- If there is media interest in the death, you may need to seek guidance from the local authority as to how to manage the television and radio crews and their requests for information and interviews.

- One of the management team may be able to act as a media liaison person. This role needs to have been considered and incorporated into the policies and procedures in order that the designated person can prepare and have training and not be put on the spot.

- Consider the potential circumstances that could arise, and build up a network of contacts that you could approach if necessary. These could include contacts in education, such as educational psychologists, and any local crisis team from the local authority or health services.

- If a school lacks training and confidence in the area of bereavement and loss, it may need to quickly seek outside help, especially if there is an element of trauma and media interest.

Exercise 20

Children attending funerals

This exercise will help participants understand the issues around children attending funerals. It should enable them to better advise and support a family seeking advice about children attending the funeral of a close relative. This may arise when contact is first made with the family. The participants can draw on their own experiences of attending funerals, especially they were children. It needs to be emphasised that people make the best decisions they can with the best information they have available. Some participants may have come to regret not letting their children attend a funeral and this needs to be addressed with tact and sensitivity. Take feedback, and once the exercise has been completed, write the results on a flipchart or whiteboard.

Exercise 20: Activity

Discuss in pairs or in a small group:

- Did you attend a funeral as a child?

- What were the circumstances?

- How did you find the experience?

- What were the positive and negative effects?

- What helped you, if anything?

- What hindered you, if anything?

- What would you do if your child or a young relative or friend wanted to go to a funeral?

- Should children attend their parent's funeral?

- Should there be any provisos, or none?

- What may help children who wish to attend?

- What advice would you give to a family who asked you whether or not the children should attend the funeral?

Reflections

- In an historical context, it is only relatively recently that children have not been actively involved in the rites of passage associated with death in their family and community. This may have included laying out the body and involvement in the funeral.

- The funeral rites after a death are a community and family event, a celebration of the life that has ceased.

- If children do not attend the funeral they are being excluded from a family rite of passage such as a wedding or a christening.

- The reality of a funeral may, with preparation, be far less worrying for children than either they or the adults anticipate.

- The 'Iceberg' research found that it was best in the long term to allow children an informed choice as to whether or not to attend the funeral of their parent.

- Children need adequate preparation before attending a funeral, and they could be taken on a prior visit to the venue, such as the church, and receive an explanation of what will happen. If children are aware of how the funeral will unfold, such as when the coffin will arrive and leave, and where it will be during the service, this will help to allay their fears.

- The same approach can be used if a crematorium is involved. Children would benefit from knowing about the proceedings, as they may assume that the coffin bursts into flames in sight at the crematorium, rather than disappearing behind curtains and being moved away.

Exercise 21

Parents, children and funerals

This exercise will help participants to gain insight into children's experiences before a funeral.One set of trainees plays the role of a parent who does not want their child to attend their partner's funeral, and the other set plays a child who wants to attend the funeral. If there are an odd numbers of trainees, have one group of three: one parent and two children. Take feedback, and once the exercise has been completed, write the results on a flipchart or whiteboard.

Prepare the following cards:

Parent

You are a parent and have arranged your partner's funeral, but you do not want your children to attend. The funeral is next Tuesday and you can choose either to refuse to let the children attend the funeral or to distract them by arranging for them to go on a trip with a relation on that day. Choose your strategy and, if necessary, defend your position to the child.

Child

You are a child and know that your parent's funeral is happening soon, possibly next Tuesday, and also that your surviving parent does not seem to want you to attend.

Try to find out the date of the funeral and then persuade your parent to let you attend.

Exercise 21: Activity

Individually, read the card you are allocated – either a parent or child card – without sharing the information with the other person.

Carry out the activity, as directed, for 5–10 minutes. Discuss in your pairs, then in a group:

• How did you feel as the parent, withholding information or consent from the child in relation to their parent's funeral?

_____

_____

_____

_____

_____

• How did you feel as the child, being refused consent to attend your parent's funeral?

_____

_____

_____

_____

_____

• Were there similarities between what others thought and felt in their pairs?

_____

_____

_____

_____

_____

Reflections

- In an historical context, it is only relatively recently that children have not been actively involved in the rites of passage associated with death in their family and community. This may have included laying out the body and involvement in the funeral.

- The funeral rites after a death are a community and family event, a celebration of the life that has ceased.

- If children do not attend the funeral, they are being excluded from a family rite of passage such as a wedding or a christening.

- The reality of a funeral may, with preparation, be far less worrying for children than either they or the adults anticipate.

- The 'Iceberg' research found that it was best in the long term to allow children an informed choice as to whether or not to attend the funeral of their parent.

- Children need adequate preparation before attending a funeral, and they could be taken on a prior visit to the venue, such as the church, and receive an explanation of what will happen. If children are aware of how the funeral will unfold, such as when the coffin will arrive and leave, and where it will be during the service, this will help to allay their fears.

- The same approach can be used if a crematorium is involved. Children would benefit from knowing about the proceedings, as they may assume that the coffin bursts into flames in sight at the crematorium, rather than disappearing behind curtains and being moved away.

Exercise 22

Children attending the chapel of rest

This exercise will help participants to be able to understand issues around children visiting the chapel of rest or seeing the body at another venue, such as in the hospital or at the deceased's home. It needs to be borne in mind that not all religions have a chapel of rest or a custom of viewing the body. This is a sensitive area, and the 'Iceberg' research showed similar results to children attending the funeral. Children are best given choice as to whether they want to see the body. If children want to see the body, it is important that they are adequately prepared. In the 'Iceberg' research, most children who chose to go to the chapel of rest did not have any problems. The exception was a small group of younger girls who were distressed by the experience.

The exercise should enable the participants to better support a family seeking advice about children viewing a body. The participants can draw on their own experiences of viewing a body, especially when they were children. It needs to be emphasised that people make the best decisions they can with the best information they have available. Some participants may have come to regret not letting their children see a body, and this needs to be addressed with tact and sensitivity. Take feedback, and once the exercise has been completed, write the results on a flipchart or whiteboard.

Exercise 22: Activity

Discuss in pairs or in a small group:

- When you were a child, did you view a body?

- How old were you at the time?

- What were the circumstances?

- How did you find the experience?

- What were the positive and negative effects?

- What helped you, if anything?

- What hindered you, if anything?

- What would you do if your child or a young relative or friend wanted to view the body?

- Should children view their parent's body?

- Should there be any provisos, or none at all?

- What might help children who wish to view a body?

- What advice would you give to a family who asked you whether or not the children should view the body?

Reflections

- In an historical context, it is only relatively recently that children have not been actively involved in the rites of passage associated with death within their family and community, including laying out and having contact with the body and attending the funeral.

- Viewing the body after a death is a more intimate family event, and not a public one like the funeral. While it is more likely that children will attend the funeral, some may want to view the body.

- The reality of viewing the body may, with preparation, be much less worrying for both the children and their parent than either they or the adults anticipate.

- The 'Iceberg' research found that it seemed best in the long term to allow children an informed choice as to whether or not to view the body of their parent.

- Seeing the body may reassure some children that the person is dead and will not be buried alive.

- Children need adequate preparation before viewing a body, including explanations as to likely changes after death. Shortly after death the body may look quite similar to when the person was alive, but after it has been prepared by the undertakers it can look quite different.

Exercise 23

Informing the school community

This exercise will help the participants to think through how staff and pupils could be told the news of a death of a parent or member of the school community. There needs to be a planned system of informing staff and pupils about the death. The timing and the method of informing staff and pupils needs to be carefully considered. The news of the death will likely already be circulating in the neighbourhood, and myths and misunderstanding can develop. Clarifying the facts and informing the school community in appropriate terms could help to reduce any misunderstandings. It is important to liaise with the family and discuss what details the school community should be told. Take feedback, and once the exercise has been completed, write the results on a flipchart or whiteboard. Ideas that emerge could be integrated into the school policy.

Exercise 22: Activity

A pupil has been bereaved. Discuss the following in pairs or a group:

- Should the school community, staff and pupils, be informed about the death?

- If yes, why?

- If no, why not?

- What are the advantages and disadvantages of telling staff and pupils?

- What details about the death should be told to staff and pupils?

- Identify those people who need to be told about the death.

- Which staff would you not tell, and why?

- How could the staff be told the news of the bereavement?

- Draw a flowchart that ensures that all those who need to know are told, and the method.

- What about staff not in school?

- What about office and ancillary staff?

- Draw a flowchart that ensures all the pupils who need to know are told, and how.

- What precautions, if any, need to be taken?

Reflections

- There could be close liaison with the family in relation to their wishes about who is told, and the pupil also needs to know who is aware of the death.

- The news will likely be circulating in the neighbourhood, and it is unrealistic that pupils will not be aware of the death, although there may be confusion and misunderstandings about what happened.

- Care needs to be taken as to how to tell staff, perhaps at a briefing, and to ensure that all ancillary staff and those not at the briefing are given sufficient information. Be prepared in case some staff are distressed and need support.

- Arrangements need to be made to ensure that all the staff – for example, those who work before school at a breakfast club, at lunchtimes and with after-school activities – are also made aware.

- Staff who are away sick or on a course, together with supply staff and new recruits, need to be kept informed, as do visitors if this is relevant and appropriate.

- How pupils are told will depend on their age and closeness to their bereaved peer. The younger children may be best told in their own classes by their own teachers, as will the bereaved pupil's friends and peers. Older pupils and those not in the same year group as bereaved pupils could perhaps be told in larger groups or in a school assembly.

- Be prepared for some pupils to become distressed and need support; have staff able to offer support, and have tissues on hand.

THE MEDIUM AND LONGER-TERM RESPONSES TO A DEATH

The following exercises move into the area of after a death or significant loss and when pupils return to school.

Exercise 24

Barriers to interacting with bereaved pupils

This exercise will help the participants to identify what may prevent them from interacting with a bereaved pupil, and if so, to reflect on how to reduce these barriers and help pupils after a significant loss. Many children find that adults are not at all approachable after a death or loss. Pupils can become isolated and have no avenues open for explanations and answers to questions that they have. The exercise uses the participants' own experiences as a basis for potentially helping pupils. Take feedback, and once the exercise has been completed, write the results on a flipchart or whiteboard.

Exercise 24: Activity

Discuss in pairs or in a small group:

- Did you experience a significant death or loss as a child?
- If yes, how easy was it for you to discuss it with teachers?
- If yes, how easy was it for you to discuss it with others?
- How did you feel at the time?
- What would have helped?
- Was there anything that you did not understand?
- Has your experience been different or the same with significant losses as an adult?
- What should you bear in mind when interacting with a bereaved pupil?
- What are the barriers to you interacting with a bereaved child?
- How could these barriers be reduced?
- What should you do if bereaved pupils tell you something that their family has told them which is confusing?
- What questions could a pupil potentially ask?
- What could you do if bereaved pupils ask you something that you do not know the answer to?

Reflections

- Liaise closely with the family and take care to observe their wishes. A good relationship could enable you to have a positive influence on the outcomes for the family and pupil.

- Death is generally a taboo subject and there could be barriers to discussing the area, especially with a pupil. Since the subject is sensitive in nature, general consent and agreement with the family is prudent, to ensure that they understand and are in agreement with the approach.

- Do not contradict what the child has been told by the family. If something causes you concern, seek a meeting with the family quickly to discuss the information given. This could relate to what a child has been told about the death, an example being that the dead parent is a 'star in the sky'.

- Do not be afraid of reaching out to a bereaved pupil and making the first tentative approach, perhaps by asking if they want to talk or by asking how you can help.

- Make time for a pupil if they want to talk with you, especially as they may have found it very difficult to make an approach. If you cannot currently make time, arrange a mutually convenient time at soon as possible. Remember that if the pupil has approached you, it indicates that they have confidence in your ability to help them.

- Being open, and discussing the area generally should help with confidence in raising the topic; you can then be guided by the response of the pupil as to whether they want to open up or close down the conversation.

- There may be a concern that mentioning the topic will distress children and young people. Research suggests the contrary and that pupils are helped by an acknowledgement of their loss. If nothing is mentioned, the pupil may think that the adult either does not know or does not care about the death.

- Pupils may be hyper-vigilant and anxious, and concerned about the welfare of the remaining parent. They may fear that the surviving parent may also die. If one parent has died, then why not the other? Their peers may also become concerned about the wellbeing of their own parents, and anxiety levels could be raised in the short term.

- Children may not want to carry on a long conversation with staff, and just need brief answers or reassurance. Adults need to be guided by how pupils respond. If they do become upset or distressed, it is important to ensure their wellbeing.

- It may be difficult to raise the subject of death with pupils, but you could start with a simple statement expressing that you are sorry to hear about the death and then go on to provide them with the opportunity of talking with you further, either then or at a later time. The words need to reflect the age and understanding of the pupil.

- There may be a view that avoiding mentioning the death will protect children. If this is an intention, then it may only be helpful in the short term, and it makes the assumption that the pupil does not want to talk. If the pupil does want to discuss things with you, by not engaging with them you are losing an opportunity to help them through the bereavement.

- Adults may underestimate children's understanding of loss and death and decide to say nothing. Children will understand explanations that are pitched at their level and experience. There is no need for explanations using complex medical terms, which may only confuse. An explanation that a part of the body is 'worn out' or 'tired' may be sufficient for a young child, and can be built on later as their understanding develops.

- There is the danger of an 'elephant in the room' situation, in that nobody will talk to anybody through fear of upsetting each other. This could mean that children and parents both want to talk to each other, but fail because of concerns that they may cause upset. The best way to break this circle is by adults making the first approach and checking if the child needs to talk.

- There may be a view that it is better that children 'don't know' about what happens after a death, and that they should not be given information. A danger with this approach is that children may feel excluded and alienated. They may also gain information through other routes, such as overhearing conversations, or from their peers. They may also make up their own myths and fantasies about the death. Ideas gained this way may not only be inaccurate, but could be far worse than the actuality. It would be best for the families to include children in discussions from the beginning, in terms that they can understand.

- Adults may be unsure of what to say after a death, especially to children. If being unsure of what to say leads to individuals not responding, the bereaved may think that they either do not know or do not care about the death.

- If someone is unsure of what to say to a bereaved person, adult or child, a good way to start is to say that you are sorry to hear about the death. The opportunity then needs to be created for the bereaved to be listened to, either then or at a time that suits them, if that is what they want. Telling pupils they can contact you later leaves the door open for them to make a further approach.

- There is a view that children are resilient and do not need help, or that somebody else can do this work. Children are not necessarily resilient and may need to talk.

- The focus needs to be on listening rather than talking and you should not be afraid of silences. You will be helping by just being present and giving help and suggestions if asked.

- Do not minimise the death or loss to the family or pupil and do not talk about positive elements relating to the bereavement, such as that the deceased is no longer in pain. If the bereaved family raises positive elements, then tactfully agree with them but with a minimal response.

- Do not give the impression that tears, being upset and sad are anything but a normal grief reaction.

- Never give the impression that you think either the family or the child could have done something different to have avoided the death, such as saying that it is a shame that the ambulance was not called earlier. The bereaved will probably already be having these thoughts.

- It is not a good idea to make over-compensatory allowances for the bereaved pupil at school as they still need the security of a structure. If there has been an issue, such as adverse behaviour, this could be discussed later with the pupil in private, but the rules need to apply. Sometimes a pupil is given a card that enables them to quietly withdraw from lessons to a safe place if they are feeling overwhelmed.

- If you have been asked a question by a bereaved pupil that you are unable to answer, then say that you do not know but will try to find out. Ask for help from others if you are unsure how to cope with a particular issue.

- Do not make a promise that you cannot keep.

- Keep all staff at school informed of matters relevant to their helping the pupil. If they do not know about significant things, then they cannot offer support to the pupil.

Exercise 25

The pupil's return to school

This exercise will help participants to reflect on how to provide a smooth transition when the pupil returns to school – that is, Golden Moment 3. The return to school needs to be carefully planned with the family and it would help if the pupil knows who is aware of the death. Pupils may return quickly to school after a death or significant loss and perhaps view school as a safe haven if their home is in turmoil. Other pupils may take longer to return, as they may need time to adjust, or they may be interested in the comings and goings at home after a death. In some cases, pupils may be reluctant to return to school as they are concerned that the remaining parent may also die or leave. Sometimes parents may prefer to have their children at home for company, at least initially. Communication with the family is important so that any issues can be discussed and addressed. Take feedback, and once the exercise has been completed, write the results on a flipchart or whiteboard.

Exercise 25: Activity 1

Discuss in pairs or in a small group your thoughts on when pupils should return to school after a death.

Answer the following questions:

- What is the optimum time that children should have off school after a death or significant loss?

- What are the issues involved?

Share your findings with a larger group. Are your views similar or different, and if so how?

Exercise 25: Activity 2

A pupil is returning to school after the death of a parent.

Discuss in pairs or in a small group:

- How do you think the pupil will be feeling?

- Reflect on any similar experiences that you have had and think how you may be able to help.

- What provisions would you make to help with the transition?

- What are the implications for policies and procedures?

Reflections

- The return of pupils to school after a death or significant loss will depend on a number of factors. Some pupils return to school quickly and others may return later for various reasons, including continued involvement in family arrangements. It is important to have a close relationship with the family and keep in touch, especially as you may be able to give advice to the family about the pupil's return.

- Sometimes children will be reluctant to return to school, especially if there is activity going on in the home, or they may have concerns that the remaining parent may also die. Pupils may be hyper-vigilant and anxious, and concerned about the welfare of the remaining parent. If one parent has died, then why not the other? Their peers may also become concerned about the wellbeing of their own parents and anxiety levels may be raised in the short term.

- Sometimes parents may encourage children to remain at home, perhaps for their own needs and company.

- The return needs to be carefully planned with the family, with decisions on the date and whether it is a sudden return or there is a transition period that tails off – for example, initially going home early or beginning school at lunchtime.

- Generally pupils will be helped by keeping to a routine, and returning to school may help. It would be a good idea to ask pupils if they have concerns and what would help them.

- Sometimes a key person, ideally chosen by the pupil, can be a source of help for them at school to provide a listening ear.

- The 'Iceberg' research showed the importance of acknowledging the loss to pupils. This needs to be done in a sensible way through staff interaction with the pupil rather than a reception committee and queue at the door! If nothing is mentioned, the pupil may think that the adult either does not know or does not care about the death.

- It may be difficult to raise the subject of death with pupils, but you could start with a simple statement expressing that you are sorry to hear about the death and then go on to provide them with the opportunity of talking with you further, either then or at a later time. The words need to reflect the age and understanding of the pupil.

- It is important that pupils are told who knows about the death – ideally everyone at school – so that they are not concerned that they may have to explain or that somebody will ask how their dead parent is.

- Do not be afraid of reaching out to a bereaved pupil and making the first tentative approach, perhaps by asking if they want to talk or by asking how you can help.

- Make time for a pupil if they want to talk with you, especially as they may have found it very difficult to make the approach. If you cannot currently make time, arrange a mutually convenient time at soon as possible. Remember that if the pupil has approached you, it indicates that they have confidence in your ability to help them.

- Being open and discussing the area generally should help with confidence in raising the topic; you can then be guided by the response of the pupil as to whether they want to open up or close down the conversation.

- Children may not want to carry on a long conversation with staff, and just need brief answers or reassurance. Adults need to be guided by how pupils respond, and if they do become upset or distressed, it is important to ensure their wellbeing.

- There may be a view that avoiding mentioning the death will protect children. If this is an intention, it may only be helpful in the short term, and it makes the assumption that the pupil does not want to talk. If the pupil does want to discuss things with you, by not engaging with them you are losing an opportunity to help them through the bereavement.

- There is a view that children are resilient and do not need help, or that somebody else can do this work. Children are not necessarily resilient and may need to talk.

- Pupils may benefit from a card that gives them permission to leave the classroom for a safe place if they are feeling overwhelmed.

- The focus needs to be on listening rather than talking. Do not be afraid of silences. You will be helping by just being present and giving help and suggestions if asked.

- Do not minimise the death or loss to the family or pupil, and do not talk about positive elements relating to the bereavement – for example, that the deceased is no longer in pain. If the bereaved family raises positive elements, then tactfully agree with them but with a minimal response.

- Do not give the impression that tears, being upset and sad are anything other than a normal grief reaction.

- Never give the impression that you think either the family or the child could have done something different to have avoided the death, such as saying that it is a shame that the ambulance was not called earlier. The bereaved will probably already be having these thoughts.

- It is not a good idea to make over-compensatory allowances for the bereaved pupil at school as they still need the security of a structure. If there has been an issue, such as adverse behaviour, then this could be discussed later with the pupil in private, but the rules need to apply.

- If you have been asked a question by a bereaved pupil that you cannot or are unable to answer, then say that you do not know but will try to find out. Ask for help from others if you are unsure how to cope with a particular issue.

- Do not make a promise that you cannot keep.

- Keep all staff at school informed of matters relevant to their helping the pupil. If they do not know about significant things, they cannot offer support to the pupil.

Exercise 26

Support for bereaved pupils

This exercise will help participants to consider potential sources of support for bereaved pupils. The Bronfenbrenner (1997) model that can be used to highlight potential support is a series of concentric rings. The closer the support is to the bull's eye, the closer it is geographically or emotionally to the pupil. The closer to the bull's eye, the greater the potential for support, but in the case of emotional closeness, those emotionally connected may also be affected by the death and not be available to pupils. This is likely not to be the case with the school and other neighbourhood and community organisations. Participants can use their own experience of gaining support in their community during a time of crisis, as well as consider their links and potential contacts that may be able to help. Take feedback, and once the exercise has been completed, write the results on a flipchart or whiteboard. Consider integrating any new ideas into the school policy.

Exercise 26: Activity

Individually, draw a series of four concentric circles as shown below but on a flipchart sized piece of paper.

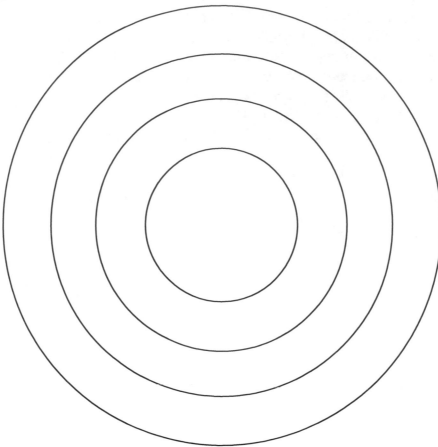

- Write your name in the bull's eye.

- Write the names of all the potential people and organisations that could support you in a crisis; the closer and more helpful they are, the closer they should be placed to the bull's eye.

- Repeat the exercise on another sheet, but this time with a 'pupil' in the bull's eye.

- Consider the potential areas of support for pupils after a bereavement.

In pairs or in a group discuss:

- Were your thoughts similar to others in the group?

- In what ways were they different or the same as others'?

Reflections

- The Bronfenbrenner notion of a network of concentric circles is relevant and helps to identify potential areas of support locally. It can also be used to identify emotional support, such as the wider family connections.

- The main potential support for bereaved pupils may be their close and immediate family, although relations may not be available to the children if they are having their own issues of grieving.

- The pupil's outer family and wider relations may also be able to offer support to pupils, although they may live some distance away and have their own issues and responsibilities. They may be important as they may be close in emotional terms to the bereaved, even if not close geographically.

- Links in the neighbourhood may be able to offer support to pupils – for example, neighbours and friends living nearby – although they may need to be activated and mobilised to help if perhaps they do not realise the need.

- Community groups and organisations in the outer circles, such as religious contacts, may also be able to offer support, as potentially could voluntary agencies, local authority and health services. The pupil may be involved in clubs or activities that are able to offer support.

Exercise 27

The 'ripple effect' after a significant death or loss 1

This exercise will help participants to understand that losses are rarely linear and one-dimensional, and encourage them to consider the potential tertiary losses. Although the presenting loss may be clearly understood, such as the death of the parent, secondary and tertiary losses may not be so clearly understood. An example is that the family may have to move house and area because of a reduction in income, which will lead to loss of their local connections and support systems. Reference could be made to the previous exercise and the Bronfenbrenner model showing blocks of support that may no longer be available after a move. Additionally, pupils may experience yet further losses that will have their own impact, such as changing schools and being unable to continue with their clubs and activities. Take feedback, and once the exercise has been completed, write the results on a flipchart or whiteboard.

Prepare the following story on a card:

Jane's story

Jane was 12 years old when her dad died. Jane had lived in a city centre since she was born, together with her parents and siblings, aged two and five years old. The family home was close to her paternal grandparents and Jane attended a large urban school where she played in the hockey team, went to her local youth club and had several close friends living nearby.

Jane's mum, who does not drive, could not afford to stay in the family house and had to move the family to live with her sister and family in a rural location 200 miles away. Jane now attends a small country school, lives in a hamlet with a handful of houses, 15 miles away from the nearest town with an infrequent bus service and no railway link.

Exercise 27: Activity

Individually, read Jane's story and consider the tertiary losses that ripple out and cause potentially unpredictable losses.

- Have you had a similar experience as a child?

  _____

- If so, how was the experience, in both positive and negative terms?

  _____

  _____

- What losses has Jane experienced so far?

  _____

  _____

- What other losses could she have experienced that are not mentioned?

  _____

  _____

- Which are the most significant losses?

  _____

  _____

- Can you think of any further potential further losses Jane could experience over time?

  _____

  _____

What implications are there for your policy and procedures?

Reflections

- Losses are likely to be multi-dimensional and have unpredictable effects beyond the presenting loss: in this case, the death of Jane's parent. Tertiary or secondary losses may flow from the initial presenting loss.

- The emotional effects of the initial loss for the pupil and their family may be amplified by these further losses.

- Tertiary losses could include a move of house, change of school, disruption of social and neighbourhood networks, loss of friendships, and loss of clubs and activities.

- There may be economic consequences if the dead parent was the main wage earner. These could include a decline in the standard of living of the family, or a move of house to cheaper accommodation.

- A move of house may involve a change of area and school for the children, who may lose friendships, leading to loss and potential isolation.

- The family and children may feel isolated in a different type of community where expectations and norms and perhaps accent are different.

- If a pupil has moved, then care could be taken to help them and their family develop links and potential support systems in the new area.

- There could be a significant change of role for pupils, such as a caring role for younger siblings; or they may be expected to take on other more adult roles, in effect losing part of their childhood.

- In the 'Iceberg' project a significant number of bereaved dads entered into new relationships within months of the mother's death, causing a further change of family dynamics and a further loss of parental availability to the children.

- In the longer term, pupils may not fully appreciate the significance of the loss until later in life, such as when the dead parent does not see them graduate or get married, or meet the grandchildren. Such family occasions that the deceased parent may miss could impact on pupils in an unexpected way.

- Bereaved pupils should be careful monitored, their needs established and their records passed on quickly to their next school.

Exercise 28

The 'ripple effect' after a significant death or loss 2

This exercise will help participants understand that losses are rarely linear and one-dimensional, and encourage them to consider the potential tertiary losses and the impact on those bereaved. This is a variation on the previous exercise, without a case study. Reference could be made to the Bronfenbrenner (1997) model, showing blocks of support that may no longer be available after a move. Take feedback, and once the exercise has been completed, write the results on a flipchart or whiteboard. Consider integrating any new ideas into the school policy.

Exercise 28: Activity

Individually:

- Recall a time when you experienced a significant amount of change: it could be moving house or a change of school.

- Draw in a circle all the other losses that you can remember from your personal life that flowed from the initial loss, such as loss of friendships.

- Now draw in another circle all the potential consequential losses that could happen after the death of a parent, and the potential economic and social effects that could affect the bereaved pupil and their family.

Share and discuss this in pairs or in a group.

Next, consider:

- What implications are there for your policy and procedures in school?

Reflections

- Losses are likely to be multi-dimensional and have unpredictable effects beyond the presenting loss. Tertiary or secondary losses may flow from the initial presenting loss. The emotional effects of the initial loss may be amplified by these further losses.

- Tertiary losses could include a move of house, change of school, disruption of social and neighbourhood networks, loss of friendships, and loss of clubs and activities.

- There may be economic consequences if the dead parent was the main wage earner. These could include a decline in the standard of living of the family, or a move of house to cheaper accommodation.

- A move of house may involve a change of area and school for the children, who may lose friendships, leading to loss and potential isolation.

- The family and children may feel isolated in a different type of community where expectations and norms and perhaps accent are different.

- If a pupil has moved, then care could be taken to help them and their family develop links and potential support systems in the new area.

- There could be a significant change of role for pupils, such as a caring role for younger siblings; or they may be expected to take on other more adult roles, in effect losing part of their childhood.

- In the 'Iceberg' project a significant number of bereaved dads entered into new relationships within months of the mother's death, causing a further change of family dynamics and a further loss of parental availability to the children.

- In the longer term, pupils may not fully appreciate the significance of the loss until later in life, such as when the dead parent does not see them graduate or get married, or meet the grandchildren. Such family occasions that the deceased parent may miss could impact on pupils in an unexpected way.

- Bereaved pupils should be careful monitored, their needs established and their records passed on quickly to their next school.

Exercise 29

Help in the medium to long term

This exercise helps participants to reflect on their experiences and consider how to help bereaved pupils in the medium to longer term after a death or significant loss. This is the time after the initial crisis when the death may not be prominent in the minds of others, but is still raw for the bereaved. There is the danger of the pupil's needs being overlooked, and adults may forget that there may be a context to issues of learning or behaviour. Pupils may find certain times difficult, such as the anniversary of the death or special occasions. Take feedback, and once the exercise has been completed, write the results on a flipchart or whiteboard.

Exercise 29: Activity

Discuss in pairs or in a small group. Think about your own experiences of bereavement:

- What has helped you after a bereavement or significant loss?

- What has hindered you after a bereavement or significant loss?

- Reflecting on your experiences, what could help pupils in the medium to longer term?

- How could school respond to pupils in the medium to longer term?

- What could be established at school? How and by whom?

- What implications are there for your policy and procedures?

Reflections

- The family is significant in supporting pupils, and continued liaison with them may help towards better outcomes for the pupil.

- Pupils may not fully understand things and be confused and reluctant to ask adults. Having a 'worry' or 'question' box could help ensure that concerns are addressed by staff. Remember to liaise with the family if asked any sensitive questions. Do not be afraid of saying that you do not know and that you will try to find out.

- Pupils may be helped by involvement in a peer support group of those who have experienced significant loss. They may feel that their emotions are better validated through peers than by adults, and this may make them feel less isolated.

- A 'loss' group could include a mix of pupils experiencing different losses, although this seems to work better when there is not too great an age gap between the pupils.

- A bereavement box such as one developed in North Suffolk and another in North Yorkshire may help schools. This contains resources held centrally and borrowed when needed by schools, although your school could develop its own. It could comprise adult-based books relating to loss and books that can be used with pupils.

- Be especially aware at anniversaries, such as the first-year anniversary of the death, on birthdays and special occasions such as Christmas, Father's and Mother's Day.

- The use of memory boxes helps pupils keep reminders and photographs in a small box. The use of a diary and writing may help some pupils express their feelings.

- Sometimes it may be appropriate to install a permanent memorial on the campus, especially if there has been a significant impact on the school community. Older pupils may take the initiative in producing temporary memorials, such as wall displays or flowers. Any ideas they have need to be treated with tact and consideration.

Exercise 30

Warning signs

This exercise helps participants consider the potential signs that a bereaved child is having difficulty in the medium and longer term. This is when the memory of the death may not be prominent in the minds of others, and it is assumed that the bereaved pupil is managing. The pupil's needs may be overlooked or misunderstood, and behaviour or learning may not be seen in the context of the loss. Most pupils will not need referral to outside agencies, but if warning signs persist, consideration should be made for outside support – ideally, links will have already been established. Take feedback, and once the exercise has been completed, write the results on a flipchart or whiteboard.

Prepare the following card:

> The parent of a bereaved pupil contacts you with concerns that they are still significantly affected by the death of their partner over a year ago and have shown little change over this time.

Exercise 30: Activity

Read the card and discuss in pairs or in a small group:

- Which warning signs would alert you, and what action would you take?

- What could you do to help and what advice would you give?

- Where could you refer the pupil if this was an option?

- What implications are there for your policy and procedures?

Reflections

- The family is at the forefront of daily interaction. They will probably be aware that the pupil is having difficulties and may seek your guidance.

- As a rule of thumb, outside agencies would not consider counselling for at least six months after bereavement in order to allow grief to take its course. The exception would be if there are other concerns, such as trauma.

- In general, if bereavement is causing significant disruption to the pupil's life after six months with no positive change, the current strategy needs to be reconsidered. However, be especially aware at anniversaries, such as that of the death, and at birthdays and special occasions such as Christmas, Father's and Mother's Day. It may be that something has triggered a temporary difficulty and that this will pass. Opportunities to listen to the pupil may help.

- Markers of potential difficulties include pupils not returning to their previous level of attainment, disorganisation, homework submitted late, demotivation, disinterest and disengagement with learning, decline in attendance, and truancy. These signs are significant if behaviour has not returned to the pre-loss level.

- Emotional warning signs include pupils becoming easily tearful, being withdrawn and 'depressed', angry and having emotional outbursts. Again, these signs are significant if behaviour has not returned to the pre-loss level.

- Pupils, especially younger ones, may become clingy to the parent, be distressed on parting, and be reluctant to leave home and interact with others.

- Pupils may be tired because of sleep difficulties – either because they are unable to sleep or are having nightmares. Behaviour may regress – for example, younger children may begin to bed-wet again, or act immature for their age.

- Pupils may engage in 'self-harm' and potentially dangerous activity. This depends on their age, and could include 'cutting', the consumption of alcohol, cigarettes, and drugs, and/or excessive risk-taking.

- Pupils may need constant reassurance and be worried about their school work.

- Pupils may show signs of anxiety, such as nail-biting, and suffer from ailments such as an stomach upsets or skin conditions.

- Friendships may have been affected, as other children may lose patience with the bereaved pupil. A bereaved teenager may engage in risky activity, as mentioned above; they may also become sexually promiscuous or lose contact with their former friends.

- The teenage years are often a time of experimentation and risk-taking, and this can be a testing stage in life for any young person and their family. In most cases, problems can be worked through, but if a bereaved teenager's behaviour seems to be spiralling out of control or you are worried and the family has not contacted you, then the first course of action would be to arrange to meet and discuss things with them. It may be that the family is unaware, or that there have been other changes at home, such as the introduction of a new partner, that may help to explain these behaviours, as the pupil may be going through further unrecognised losses.

- Where possible, interventions should be discussed with the family beforehand, to help keep a positive relationship, and avoid them being surprised if they are later made aware by the pupil.

- Pupils could well benefit from being asked if they would like anybody to listen to them.

- Liaise with the family if you are asked sensitive questions by a pupil, and do not be afraid of saying that you do not know or that you will try to find out, for example the specifics of how their parent died.

- Pupils can be helped by involvement in a peer support group of those who have gone through a similar experience. Pupils may feel their emotions are better validated through their peers than through adults and may thus feel less isolated and different.

- A 'loss' group could also include a mix of pupils having experienced different losses, although groups seem to work better when there is not too great an age range.

- In terms of onward referral, this will depend on the nature of the difficulty. The pupil's GP could be a port of call if there is a health issue, and contacts that you have already established, such as the educational psychologist, may be able to give informal advice and guidance.

Exercise 31

Bereavement policy and procedure

This final exercise is designed to help participants develop ideas for the school policy. Ideally, it should be done after being primed by the previous exercises. First, explain the idea of the Golden Moments to the participants and ensure that they understand their importance (see Chapter 1).

The ideas developed in the training process can be brought together to form a coherent policy or procedure for your school that responds to the predicted needs of pupils after a death and also has the flexibility to respond to unforeseen circumstances. The headings could include how to respond to the family, and what is needed in school after the death, when the pupil returns to school, and in the longer term. It is important that the policy is relevant to the context of the school, and ideally it is assembled integrating the views of all the staff as far as possible. Take feedback, and once the exercise has been completed, write the results on a flipchart or whiteboard.

Exercise 31: Activity

Discuss in pairs or groups what could be included in a bereavement policy or procedure:

- What are the general headings needed in a bereavement policy or procedure?
- What needs to be in place, especially bearing in mind the Golden Moments?
  - Golden Moment 1: Receiving the news of the death
  - Golden Moment 2: The funeral
  - Golden Moment 3: The return to school
  - Golden Moment 4: Change of class or school
- How could these be integrated into a coherent policy?
- What implications are there for your current policy and procedures?

Reflections

Points that could be considered:

- Who will make the initial contact with the family?

- What if the school hears the news of the death indirectly and has not been contacted by the family?

- Are there any religious or cultural implications? How could these be identified?

- How will the initial contact be made (perhaps by telephone or with a follow-up visit)?

- How will the contact be continued and maintained?

- How will the school respond to the family?

- What information about the death is needed, and who needs to know?

- Do the other pupils need to know, and how will they be told?

- How can pupils who are emotionally affected by the death be identified, such as close friends or other pupils who have been bereaved?

- What role can governors play in supporting the school?

- What outside agencies and neighbourhood organisations could be mobilised to support the family?

- How can the pupil's transition back to school be planned and monitored?

- What reactive processes can be put in place to support pupils, and what techniques can be used?

- Can death or loss education be included in the curriculum?

- How can records be passed between classes and schools? How can important dates and anniversaries be addressed?

- How can pupils be monitored over time?

- Who will be responsible for identifying training needs and developing and monitoring loss training, and in what timescale?

- Who will be responsible overall for developing a policy? Who will be consulted in its development, and how and when will it be reviewed?

Supporting Bereaved Pupils: A Summary

ADAPTING THE LESSONS OF BEREAVEMENT TO LOSS GENERALLY

The focus on the exercises has related to the bereavement of a pupil. Staff at school may also experience bereavement, and the exercises can be adapted relatively simply.

Pupils may experience a series of losses, including parental separation and divorce, disability, the imprisonment of a parent, being in 'public care', neglect or abuse, ill-health or having a parent or family member seriously ill, the death of a pet, move of house and area, and change of school.

Equally, staff at school may experience their own losses, including the death of parents or a child, separation and divorce, ill-health, redundancy and retirement.

The strategies and policies in place should alert you to the potential effects and can guide you in terms of responding, putting effective communication in place and having a humane and human approach.

Some guiding principles

- Any death, especially that of a parent, can be a challenging and confusing time for children, young people and adults, including staff at school. Confusion is not necessarily restricted to those who have been bereaved.

- The adults in the immediate family will be going through their own grieving process, and this may mean that they are unable to facilitate the grief of their children.

- The school community can be a significant part of the pupil's support network, and has the potential to offer crisis support to their family as well.

- There is a potentially wide network of support that could be mobilised to help pupils, including organisations within the local community.

- The death of a parent involves more than the presenting loss. The ripples of the effects of the death can be far-reaching and unpredictable; they can flow over time and affect the bereaved years later. Loss is multi-dimensional, despite often being seen as one-dimensional with a single solution.

- There is a body of research showing the potential adverse effects on children and young people after a parental death. These include effects on their attainment at school and their life chances, as well as on their behaviour. Responding to a pupil's needs can be seen in this context.

- Many losses can affect children and young people, including separation, the death of grandparents or siblings, disability, parental imprisonment, transitions between phases and classes in school, moves of house and the death of pets.

- There are potentially four Golden Moments that could be key in supporting children and young people. Schools are well placed to play a significant part, especially if there is close liaison throughout with the family. If these Golden Moments are addressed, they may have a significant and positive impact on pupils.

- Schools need staff to be aware of a pupil's needs after a loss, and have the power to implement changes and put strategies in place. Both awareness and power are needed to enable effective responses.

Useful Resources

Serendipity

We live in a changing world, and children may encounter loss and death in their everyday lives, such as a pet dying or finding a dead hedgehog on the road. These are opportunities for children to raise issues of loss and death naturally and they should not be discouraged from asking questions that will help them to gain a better idea of the cycle of life.

Observing life cycles such as butterflies developing from eggs and frogs from frog spawn may help children to gain an idea of life's changes, although they may need to be explicitly guided to see change as loss and death, such as leaf fall in winter and new leaves in spring.

Further reading

You may be asked by parents or colleagues for books for further reading or to add to a school library. Here are some suggestions:

Understanding Children's Experiences of Parental Bereavement by the author (published by Jessica Kingsley 2001) is an ideal companion book, being based on doctoral research into the experiences of children after the death of a parent, which has been used to underpin interventions.

Talking about Death and Bereavement in School by Ann Chadwick (published by Jessica Kingsley 2012) gives insights into communicating with children of primary school age.

What Does Dead Mean? by Caroline Jay and Jenni Thomas (published by Jessica Kingsley 2012) is a book for children and adults able to discuss what death means.

A Teacher's Handbook of Death by Maggie Jackson and Jim Colwell (published by Jessica Kingsley 2001) gives ideas of how to talk with children about death.

Great Answers to Difficult Questions about Death by Linda Goldman (published by Jessica Kingsley 2009) and *Great Answers to Difficult Questions about Divorce* by Fanny Cohen Herlem (published by Jessica Kingsley 2008) are both books that offer ideas for talking with children, probably better used by parents and carers when interacting with children.

Children Also Grieve: Talking about Death and Healing by Linda Goldman (published by Jessica Kingsley 2003) can be used to help children work through and understand issues with adult support.

Not Now Bernard by David McKee (published by Anderson Press 2012) is an interesting fictional book picture about communication for younger children, and *It's Raining Cats and Dogs* by Michael Barton (published by Jessica Kingsley 2011) gives insight into the potential confusion and misunderstanding that can be caused by the English language.

Muddles, Puddles and Sunshine by Diana Crossley and Kate Sheppard (published by Hawthorn Press 2010) is an activity book that children can work through with parents after a death. Engaging in activities can help children to more easily share their thoughts and concerns.

Books such as *Dogger* by Shirley Hughes (published by Red Fox 2009) can help children to think about and discuss loss, in this case the loss of a favourite toy.

Michael Rosen's Sad Book by Michael Rosen and Quentin Blake (published by Walker Books 2011), exploring sadness in bereavement, could be useful for teenagers.

Waterbugs and Dragonflies: Explaining Death to Young Children by Doris Stickney (published by Pilgrim Press 2004) can be used for younger children, this being a life cycle book; also, *Heaven* by Nicholas Allan (published by Red Fox 2014), about the death of a pet, may be suitable for younger children.

Appropriate text books in relation to biology may help children initially gain an idea of life cycles, and other subjects, such as history or English literature, potentially provide similar opportunities.

Books can potentially be positive resources for children, although it is important to actively engage with them and ensure that they understand the content and are deriving benefit from the book. Children should not just be left to read a book in isolation in the expectation that they will necessarily gain understanding.

Metaphors may not be apparent to children and may need explaining.

Grief in the Family, a DVD by Leeds Animation Workshop (2002), is a useful short film for professionals to gain insight and could be used in combination with other training.

Films such as the *Lion King* (Disney 1994) and *Finding Nemo* (Disney 2003) can also help children gain insights, but metaphors and links may need to be explained.

Bibliography

Bandura, A. (1962) *Social Learning Through Imitation*. Lincoln, NE: University of Nebraska Press.

Berg, I., Rostila, M., Saarela, J. and Hern, A. (2014) 'Parental death during childhood and subsequent school performance.' *Journal of the American Academy of Paediatrics, 133*, 4, 682–9.

Blackburn, M. (1991) 'Bereaved children and their teachers.' *Bereavement Care 10*, 2, 19–21

Bowlby, J. (1963) 'Pathological mourning and childhood mourning.' *Journal of the American Psycho-analytical Association, 11*, 500–10.

Bowlby, J. (1981) *Attachment and Loss: Loss, Sadness and Depression* (vol 3). New York, NY: Basic Books.

Bronfenbrenner, U. (1979) *The Ecology of Human Development: Experiments by Nature and Design*. Cambridge, MA: Harvard University Press.

Bronfenbrenner, U. (1997) 'Human Ecological Models of Human Development.' In M. Gauvin and M. Cole (eds) *Readings in the Development of Children* (2nd edn). New York, NY: W. H. Freeman and Company.

Chadwick, A. (2012) *Talking About Death and Bereavement in School*. London: Jessica Kingsley Publishers.

Chaiklin, S. (2003) 'The Zone of Proximal Development in Vygotsky's Analysis of Learning and Instruction.' In A. Kozulin, B. Gindis, B. V. Ageyev and S. Miller (eds) *Vygotsky's Educational Theory and Practice in Cultural Context*. Cambridge: Cambridge University Press.

Cross, S. (ed.) (2005) *'I Can't Stop Feeling Sad': Calls to ChildLine about Bereavement*. London: ChildLine Publications.

Dyregov, A. (1991) *Grief in Children: A Handbook for Adults*. London: Jessica Kingsley Publishers.

Fox, S. (1985) *Good Grief: Helping Groups of Children When a Friend Dies*. Boston: New England Association for the Education of Young Children.

Goldman, L. (2002) *Breaking the Silence: A Guide to Help Children with Complicated Grief*. Philadelphia, PA: Brunner-Routledge.

Goldman, L. (2014) *Life and Loss: A Guide to Help Grieving Children*. Hove: Routledge.

Harrison, L. and Harrington, R. (2001) 'Adolescents' bereavement experiences. Prevalence, association with depressive symptoms, and use of services.' *Journal of Adolescence, 24*, 159–69.

Holland, J. M. (1993) 'Child bereavement in Humberside.' *Educational Research, 35*, 3, 289–97.

Holland, J. M. (2001) *Understanding Children's Experience of Parental Bereavement*. London: Jessica Kingsley Publishers.

Holland, J. (2004) 'Should children attend their parents' funerals?' *Pastoral Care in Education, 22*, 10–14.

Holland, J., Dance, R., MacManus, N. and Stitt, C. (2005) *Lost for Words: Loss and Bereavement Awareness Training Pack for Adults*. London: Jessica Kingsley.

Holland, J. and McLennan, D. (2015a) 'North Yorkshire schools' responses to pupil bereavement.' *Pastoral Care in Education, 33*, 2, 116–28.

Holland, J. and Wilkinson, S. (2015b) 'A comparative study of the child bereavement response and needs of schools in North Suffolk and Hull, Yorkshire.' *Bereavement Care, 34*, 2, 55–58.

Kubler-Ross, E. (1980) *On Death and Dying*. London: Tavistock Publications.

Lowton, K. and Higginson, I. J. (2003) 'Managing bereavement in the classroom: A conspiracy of silence?' *Death Studies, 27*, 717–41.

Mallon, B. (1997) *Helping Children to Manage Loss*. London: Jessica Kingsley.

McGuinness, B. (2009) 'Grief in the workplace.' *Bereavement Care, 28*, 1, 2–8.

Oyebode, J. R. and Owens, R. G. (2013) 'Bereavement and the role of religious and cultural factors.' *Bereavement Care, 32*, 2, 60–4.

Purdy, N. (2013) *Pastoral Care: A Critical Introduction*. London: Bloomsbury.

Ribbens McCarthy, J. and Jessop, J. (2005) *Young People, Bereavement and Loss*. London: National Children's Bureau.

Rowlings, L. and Holland, J. (2000) 'A comparative study of grief and suicide in English and Australian Schools.' *Death Studies, 24*, 35–50.

Stroebe, M. and Schut, H. (1999) 'The dual process model of coping with bereavement: Rationale and description.' *Death Studies, 23*, 197–224.

Till, A. (ed.) (1994) *The Collected Poems of William Wordsworth*. Ware, Hertfordshire: Wordsworth Editions Publishers.

Tracey, A. (2006) 'Perpetual Loss and Pervasive Grief. An Exploration of the Experiences of Daughters Bereaved of their Mother in Early Life.' PhD dissertation. Londonderry: University of Ulster, Magee.

Tracey, A. and Holland, J. (2008) 'A comparative study of child bereavement and loss responses and needs of schools in Hull, Yorkshire and Derry/Londonderry, Northern Ireland.' *Pastoral Care in Education, 26*, 4, 253–66.

Vygotsky, L.S. (1978) *Mind in Society: The Development of Higher Psychological Processes*. Cambridge, MA: Harvard University Press.

John Holland's Publications

1993 'Child bereavement in Humberside.' *Educational Research, 35*, 3, 289–97.

1994 'Bereavement in the classroom.' *National Federation for Educational Research* 'Topic Resource Pack' Package No 12.

1995 'The effects of bereavement on children in Humberside secondary schools', with Corinne Ludford. *British Journal of Special Education, 22*, 2, 56–9.

1997 'Child bereavement in Humberside schools.' *Bereavement Care, 16*, 1, 8–10.

1997 *Coping with Bereavement: A Handbook for Teachers*. Cardiff: Cardiff Academic Press.

1999 'Children and the Impact of Parental Death.' Doctoral research project at the University of York (Operation 'Iceberg').

2000 'A comparative study of grief and suicide in English and Australian schools', with Louise Rowling, University of Sydney. *Death Studies, 24*, 35–50.

2000 'Secondary schools and pupil loss by parental bereavement and parental relationship separations.' *Pastoral Care in Education, 18*, 4, 39.

2001 *Understanding Children's Experiences of Parental Bereavement*. London: Jessica Kingsley.

2003 'Supporting schools with loss: "Lost for Words" in Hull.' *British Journal of Special Education, 30*, 2, 76–8.

2004 'Should children attend their parents' funerals?' *Pastoral Care in Education, 22*, 1, 10–14.

2004 *Loss in Schools*. National Federation for Educational Research 'Topic Resource Pack', March.

2004 'Lost for Words in Hull.' *Pastoral Care in Education, 22*, 4, 10–14.

2005 *Lost for Words: Loss and Bereavement Awareness Training Pack for Adults*, with Ruth Dance, Nic McManus and Carole Stitt. London: Jessica Kingsley.

2005 *Supporting Children in Public Care in Schools: A Resource for Trainers of Teachers, Carers and Social Workers*, with Catherine Randerson. London: Jessica Kingsley.

2008 'How schools can support children who experience loss and death.' *British Journal of Guidance and Counselling, 36*, 4, 411–24.

2008 'A comparative study of the child bereavement and loss responses and needs of schools in Hull, Yorkshire and Derry/Londonderry, Northern Ireland', with Anne Tracey. *Pastoral Care in Education, 26*, 4, 253–66.

2009 'Children Should Be Seen and not Heard', with Janis Hostad. In Lorna Foyle and Janis Hostad Radcliffe (eds) *Illuminating the Diversity in Cancer and Palliative Care*. Oxford: Radcliffe Publishing Limited.

2015 'North Yorkshire schools' responses to pupil bereavement', with Derek McLennan. *Pastoral Care in Education*, *33*, 2, 116–128.

2015 'A comparative study of the child bereavement response and needs of schools in North Suffolk and Hull, Yorkshire', with Susan Wilkinson. *Bereavement Care*, *34*, 2, 55–58.